JOSEPH CONRAD AND THE WEST

JOSEPH CONRAD AND THE WEST
Signs of Empire

Jacques Darras

Translated from the French
by Anne Luyat and Jacques Darras

BARNES & NOBLE BOOKS
TOTOWA, NEW JERSEY

For Anne-Marie

First published in the U.S.A. 1982 by
BARNES & NOBLE BOOKS
81, Adams Drive, Totowa
New Jersey, 07512
ISBN 0–389–20071–9

Printed in Hong Kong

Contents

1 Introduction

In his preface to *The Tales of Unrest*[1], Joseph Conrad told the story of the pen he used to write his short story 'The Lagoon'. Wishing to put the instrument in a place of safekeeping, he entrusted it to a wooden salad bowl which also contained a variety of other domestic objects. One day, in the course of one of his regular inspections, he was surprised to discover not one but two pens! Not knowing which one should be the object of his solicitude, and rather than make a favourite of the one that meant nothing to him, he decided to dispose of both of them. Thrown from a window, their flight followed a rhetorical parabola of the most pertinent kind and let them fall to earth in a flower bed, the ideal poetic tomb. Although it would be most audacious to make critical assumptions on the strength of such a seemingly insignificant incident, it is possible to compare this modest fiction and Conrad's methods of composition. A pen which becomes two pens as soon as its purpose is fulfilled, a pen which meets a sister soul in the bottom of a salad bowl – an epic helmet (in a picaresque inn) which has been turned over to become a recipient for sealing wax and for the links of broken chains – could this not be an amusing parallel for the mysterious and romantic image which was an obsession with Conrad, that of the secret sharer? Too much ink has already been spilled on this subject for us not to be intrigued by the possibility of clarifying it at last. That the pen be thus promoted to the rank of actor, that it leave behind the secondary role to which it had been confined behind the scenes of the play to take its place on the stage is one way of indicating, without being too obvious about it, the importance he gives to the writing itself. The fact that the pen appears in the author's memory in the form of a sentimental whim should not make us forget the dual relation which makes of the writer – in the secret corners of his mind, in his efforts to escape from himself – his own reader, both double and hypocrite. A pen divided in two is, after all, the sign of an even more intimate duplicity, of a fission running through the stories like an imperceptible tremor. If we want the secret sharer to be the other

I

side of the personality to which we are chained in the passivity of the night, the visitor of the night come to disturb the sleep of the just man, we cannot affirm that its more active intervention does not intermingle with another one – that of the language itself, of the real 'Secret Agent'. If we look beyond the psychological chasm where waves of Victorian ink, the chaotic colour of midnight-blue, continue to cascade, shall we not encounter the source of a more essential duality which both brings together and separates the currents of the statement and its expression? A pen endowed with a double, beyond the ethical opposition to which the ambiguity of Conrad's writing has for far too long been confined, appears the couple of a more fundamental alienation which incessantly detaches the active word from the myth which it is supposed to reanimate. Impossible the confusion, eternal the repetition; each living flourish of the writing has as its double the minuscule 'colossus', a monument to dead words,[2] that the hand hastens in one gesture to write – and to obliterate.

What a fuss, you may say, for one or two pens which the author hastily disposed of in a flower bed – the ideal poetic depository for the vestiges of his past. We could reply, quite justly, that in his prefaces Conrad buries himself with a lightness of heart which is deceptive and that he sends himself 'posthumous' flowers whose real meaning we do not always fully appreciate. The quotation 'to render the highest kind of justice to the visible universe' is culled regularly from the Preface of Prefaces (*The Nigger of the Narcissus*) to grace the headings of anthologies. And while we are on the subject of flowers, do not forget that under the narcissus hides a Negro, a slave to the rhetoric, a mad Negro polishing, without rhyme or reason, his one-penny gems. He has the blind task, in the obscure prison constituted by writing where the condemned worker is enchained, of making us hear, of making us feel and, above all, of making us see. His is a blind task carried out in the obscure confinement of darkest Africa, from which he extracts the raw materials of his art in order to deploy them under 'Western Eyes'. Is he a 'nigger', a slave labourer slavering over an exotic literary cuisine for the jaded palates of his masters, who continually demand more and more spices? And what if the master chef added, from time to time, just a dash of poison, one too small to be noticed but which would have its effect in the long run? Is it not characteristic of the servant to imitate the actions of his masters and to know how to hide the greatest divergence from the norm under the appearance of the

most absolute conformity? Conrad's fiction conforms to a traditional taste for spices. His first readers did not have the faintest idea
that there was any trace of poison and did not feel at first the
burning sensation produced by the explosive mixture of spices, by
all the heavy Malay sweets. On the contrary, they were carried off
by this acquired taste, to the furthest reaches of the Orient. The
Judeas which exploded with cargoes of coal from Newcastle, the
foyers where cooks and not the dinner were roasted, made a
prodigious smokescreen behind which, urged on by their whetted
appetites, the Victorians of the colonial era imagined some ultimate
sweetmeat, some tempting apple on a breadfruit tree. And the final
deception, far from leaving a bitter taste in the mouth, giving as it
did only a conventional foretaste of the peace which surpasses our
understanding (*shantih!*), appeared to be a wise provision of water
for those dry, parched mouths.

A ghost-writer chasing after chimeras, you may say, a transfer of
damnation carried out under a romantic banner! Is it not like
looking for a diabolic quality in Conrad's work, like bringing
together two traditions, that of the vampire stealing blood and that
of the clever genie creating illusions? To which we could reply that a
certain form of duplicity is attested to by the author himself and that
this foreigner who acquired British nationality never really became
a British subject, but chose the least constraining type of mask
possible in order to remain perfectly free behind his respectable
façade. It is certainly not by accident that Conrad declared that he
was more English than his contemporaries but also less
nationalistic. Speaking of another writer and contemporary,
Rudyard Kipling, to whom he was so often linked under the yoke of
the Empire, he defines very subtly the difference which separates
their work, and by means of this definition puts himself outside all
known national boundaries. According to Conrad, Kipling adapts
all the more easily to foreign traditions because his principal interest
is in the subject itself, in its content, which means that he loses
nothing at all by changing his 'vehicle', small or large, as long as the
direction taken stays the same – on a straight course for the Orient.[3]
In contrast to Kipling's poverty in so far as language is concerned –
his stories reel off their content in many different time-belts –
language is part and parcel of Conrad's writing and contributes to
create its unique quality. It is true that this foreigner converted to
English late in life is not as sensitive to the mediating aspects of his
instrument as to its final effects and that his language seems to be

destined not so much for translation as for duplicity.

Language is a two-sided coin for him, a currency that can no longer be exchanged in the markets of the world like the solid sterling pound had been until then. Taken out of circulation and no longer convertible, language devaluates the reality that it had been given the task of valorising and manipulates all the transactions for its own benefit. But this movement only represents one phase; it is not a question, either, of a desire to save money, to refine the language, 'to give a purer meaning to the words of the tribe', or to constitute a 'cash reserve' in the manner of the Third Republic in order to be prepared for all kinds of vulgar crises. In other words, Conrad is continually putting us off on a false track; he continues to give the colour of saffron to his stories and to intersperse his sentences with flakes of gold while showing us the 'Nigger' at work in the shop of the counterfeiter, stamping the image of the queen, the stamp of *Victory* on the reverse side of the Jubilee coins. And this practice is all the more difficult to analyse since it takes place under the cover of what it proposes to expose, and is a preliminary, so to speak, which avoids the outrageous as well as the imperceptible. In nautical terms, we could speak of coastal navigation, of staying as close as possible to the land, which must be avoided at all costs. That is why it would be useless to look for another origin for the author apart from his own writing, for he was less anxious about the points of anchorage than about the effect which the writing produces. That is why it is quite absurd to look for them, as some persist in doing, out of cultural nationalism, in the country called Poland. Inversely, because he chose English for writing, we must not conclude that Conrad became an Englishman. All of this is clearly indicated in a letter to a Polish reader who had just completed the first article ever written about him in a French revue: 'The "homo duplex" has, in my case, more than one meaning. You understand, of course. I need not go into the question.'[4]

It is not really certain however that this first reader, in spite of his merit, really was as much of an accomplice as Conrad made him out to be. Speaking from the pages of a French literary review about a writer whom the French language had fashioned long before the English impose had, this Pole expressed his surprise that in his books Conrad was more sympathetic to the British government's point of view than that of the other European powers, especially France.[5] The Pole also remarked that the emblems of colonial absurdity chosen by Conrad, such as the French warship in 'Heart of

Darkness', which sent its miserable salvoes into the nothingness of
the African continent, revealed favouritism on his part. To which
Conrad replied that any other nation could just as well have been
implicated in the incident and that, as it turned out, the ship he had
actually encountered in Africa was a French one engaged in the
'War of Dahomey'.[6] Is this not one more proof that Conrad
depicted reality with a great degree of faithfulness? He even
remembered the name of the ship, the *Seignelay*. This ultimate
precision, this final touch which brings its guarantee of truth to the
incertitudes of fiction, is a curious one, to say the least. Let us look at
it from another angle. Is it not really the one last drop which makes
the vase overflow – or the ship sink – the one last drop of water or
even one last drop of blood in the process of some linguistic
transubstantiation? *Seignelay*, '*saigne-les*', bleed them. Conrad is
planting his anarchistic disorder where reality and fiction meet,
confident that the confusion produced will protect him. Besides,
such a tactic would not be incompatible with his official declar-
ations concerning romanesque legitimacy which demanded for art
the right to deform, at least to a certain degree, real experience and
actual facts. It is not impossible that his apparent fidelity to reality is
destined to disconcert his readers, that it is an ironic challenge
behind the most solid appearances, behind the most solid figures. Of
Marlow, the narrator of several of his stories, Conrad notes
complaisantly that the critics have made him in turn a 'clever
screen', 'a simple expedient', 'a figurehead', 'a familiar sprite', and
'a whispering demon'[7] – that is to say, a great many wide-ranging
interpretations which are all the more radical in their well-meaning
neutrality. Now the flippant remark of Conrad that no one, to his
knowledge, 'had ever hinted that Marlow was anything but a
gentleman'[8] raises by the very incongruity of its nature, certain
doubts. His expression of satisfaction and surprise that no exegete
had ever formulated the discourteous hypothesis of 'fraudulent'
intentions of 'charlatanism' concerning Marlow makes one immediately suspicious and brings to the forefront of the mind a
certain mistrust which, until that moment, had been dormant. It
seems that a kind of secret jubilation, an almost imperceptible
hairline fracture, is to be found at the heart of Conrad's sentences.
We are constantly presented with the temptation of 'otherness' with
which to complicate the simplicity of the apparent signification; the
shadow or the double denies the evidence of the light. Is it
ponderous of the author to declare that it is his responsibility, unless

it weighs on him or unless it be question of a lie 'it lies on me to confess'[9] that he was during the course of his double life – 'all my two lives' – adopted and spoiled by the Empire? Ponderous or not, we believe that Conrad diverges constantly from the norm and prefers discreet dissimulation to brazen eccentricity. Whether amalgam or integration, the process entails a major risk – that of confusion. In conforming to the customs of his adopted country, Conrad exposes himself to misunderstanding. A beloved spoiled child of the British Empire, certainly, but also a child spoiled by the founders of the colonial enterprise to whom, as an orphan, he had come, seeking his identity. Joseph Conrad chose an exile of ambiguous ingratitude, the spoiled child suffering from his spoilations.

Conrad's artistic duplicity is marked by a secret determination to surpass reality imperceptibly in his fiction, to carry his moderate opposition to the very heart of the language. It is translated in the narrative schema by a variety of dual relationships. As he takes care to point out, he does not write, like Kipling, about the English, but rather for the English.[10] That is to say, his exclusion, his exile in the midst of a society whose language he does not really speak (the testimony in letters and in fiction, from Conrad, on this point, could not be more eloquent), would lead us to suppose that he was formerly a member of good standing. What an uncomfortable position for someone who had come to 'convert' the British Isles, bringing with him the breviary of French novel-writing and meeting barbarians like H. G. Wells, a faithful practitioner of direct narration,[11] who were happy in their ignorance. He finds himself obliged to conform to existing literary criteria, all the while trying, by means of his art, to make subtle changes in those standards. That he was able to lead this double life is due in great part to the fact that he respects rigorously the limits of the novel form. In considering a subtle work of fiction like 'Heart of Darkness' we could regret that a more virulent attack, in the form of a pamphlet perhaps, something with a more immediate effect, had not been written in its place. There is a certain irony in the fact that 'Heart of Darkness' has been described as prophetic by several successive generations of ethnologists and historians, when really it was written at its appointed time in history.[12] In this story, the political aspect of the writing is masked by the apparent conformity of the text and by this means keeps its distance from history as such. What Conrad's pen obliterates is the closed circuit of adolescent literature from which the British Empire drew and furnished its models. What dies in *Lord Jim* is the identifiable hero. A hero is born who does not fulfil the expectations of the works which try and annex him. What disappears with Kurtz is the noble hero and the hypothesis that the colonial quest was undertaken for the purest of reasons. Already, in these first works, the most romantic ones, the most openly exotic ones, there is a divorce between the White dream of progress and the Oriental mystique which the members of the White race, in the depths of their hearts, had promised themselves to conquer.

When all is said and done, isn't the myth of origins, of youth, simply a sinister comedy played around a table by teary-eyed old men reliving their souvenirs and warming palates which have been jaded by too many Oriental spices? For these loosened tongues Conrad fashions a fork – diabolic tongues running after their problematic unity. Like these starcrossed words, like these crossed-out words with which an invisible copyist flowers the discourse of the incorrigible gossip Marlow, who himself looks for the wavering image of old acquaintances in the dark reflections of the Bordeaux wine. Like this double voice – or double truth – which comes out of the 'Heart of Darkness', borrowing, in order to make itself understood to those men of London, the nonplussed voice of their colleague Marlow. However this sober speech which is audible in the romantic raptures of inebriety, does not constitute its legitimacy because of its negative virtues, but is inseparable from the myth which it criticises and which it shelters, in much the same way as the author Joseph Conrad is a prisoner of that England from which he excludes himself by his art. Never does the foreign writer judge himself to be superior to the instrument which permits him 'to live by the pen' not only materially, but also poetically, because that instrument is his only contact with the world. In his case, duplicity springs from a fundamental duality inherent in- his practice of writing. Should we see in Joseph Conrad a kind of Razumov, prisoner of a fictional Switzerland, half way between the functionalism of English practicality satisfied with the factual truth of journalism and a Russia under the yoke of its tyrannical fictions?[13] Is Switzerland a land of exile, of speechlessness and of deafness? Is it a stage where historic gestures are imitated on the screen of writing? Is it the centre of Europe and of the world where the writer's universe is just a little off-centre?

Part I
Mythical East

2 An Intoxicating Tale

THE TARNISHED BLAZON

You might say that 'Youth' wears its symbols on its sleeve much as the *Judea* has its motto painted on its hull: 'There was below her name in big letters a lot of scrollwork with the gilt off and some sort of a coat of arms with the motto "Do or Die" underneath.' (p. 5.) The name and the motto are not mere flourishes or ornaments of the text but rather emblems waiting to be deciphered. Scrollwork, far from being an irrelevant word here, is pertinent and quite illuminating. It is easy to understand why Conrad changed the real name of the ship he had sailed on, the *Palestine*, to the *Judea*, for Judea not only conjures up visions of the Bible but also points to a favourite theme of romance, that of the Wandering Jew. Now, what Marlow exposes in his narration, without realising it, are the hazards of such an enterprise. Fascinated as he is by the blazing light of 'Youth', Marlow concentrates all his attention on recapturing the light he saw in the past. Attempting to rekindle the sparks of a long-forgotten past in his listeners, Marlow warms to his subject but does not seem to be aware of the shadows which gather behind his fiery narrative. And yet the shadows are as real as the ship's great age, which is perfectly visible in spite of a new coat of paint. Like the *Judea*, 'Youth' is old, as old as the hills and Herod; it is a leaky story which all the pilot's skill can barely keep afloat. Like the tarnished blazon on the hull of the *Judea*, its gilt has been rubbed off. The ship is not the only old thing found in the story, for the crew members also have something historic, and even Biblical, about them. Witness the symbolic quality of the mate's name: ' . . . and his name was Mahon but he insisted that it should be pronounced Mann'. Witness the skipper, Captain Beard, who has one of the classic attributes of a patriarch if only in name. Witness the steward who answers to the Biblical name of Abraham. This is not so much a ship then as an ark, and we can easily predict that Marlow's enterprise will be hampered more by the weight of tradition than by anything else. Yet, we should also take into consideration that the weight is lessened in so far as not only the gilt but the guilt, too, has been rubbed off. In other words the story really has no definite connection with the *New Testament*, for, although the fire that returns the old carcass of a ship into nothingness will have the same purifying effect as any Biblical fire, we are closer here to an epic tradition from which sin and guilt are absent. What is the meaning of the conflagration if not to warn us that in order to reach the East and to step into the marvellous world of fables we must first set fire to the *Judea* and dissipate the shadow which it casts. The origin of the story lies beyond good and evil, beyond sin and guilt. Before setting out, we must throw overboard all the guilt/gilt which weighs down the Western ark and go to the very end of the road opened by the Romantics, far beyond the mythic country where the Jews continue to wander under the same old curse. Unknowingly, it is Marlow who acts as the fire-robber, as the diverter of symbols. Let us take the example of the pillar of fire which, in the time of Abraham, was sent down to devastate the cities of Sodom and Gomorrah. In this story, it ascends instead of descending, propelling Marlow upwards towards the heavens in what can only be described as a parody of a celestial phenomenon: 'No doubt about it – I was in the air and my body was describing a sort of parabola.' We should not forget, either, that before being sent into the air Marlow happened to be standing within a few feet of the carpenter, which is an ironic coincidence indeed. When the coal in the hold explodes and tears the decks apart, it makes the foundations of the heavenly universe tremble. The carpenter in charge of maintaining the floating nave is helpless and cannot do anything when he sees his bench turned upside-down by the explosion. It is not only his bench, of course, but one which represents all the benches where crosses have been fashioned or where sentences have been handed down by inquisitors. On that ship of fools – in the image of an inverted universe – Marlow first ascends into Heaven and then descends into Hell, where he immediately falls headlong on to a layer of burning cinders, for the hell which had been contained until then in the hold spreads suddenly and without warning. The crew, a gang of Liverpool thieves, whose past had not been treated by Conrad until that moment, undergo, successfully, a kind of baptism by fire. Then the reader is a witness to a series of startling metamorphoses that could have come out of a medieval bestiary. The helmsman who fell overboard catches up with the ship, after swimming in the water with lusty strokes like some kind of merman. All the guilty animals who were not allowed on Noah's ark turn up again. The apotheosis of this hell-like atmosphere is the crew's last supper amidst the flames. Like a satanic master of ceremonies, Mahon, the first mate with the aquiline profile, presides over the feast:

> Mahon got up. With his handsome and disreputable head, his hooked profile, his long white beard and with one uncorked bottle in his hand he resembled one of those reckless sea-robbers of old making merry amidst the violence and disaster. 'The last meal on board,' he explained solemnly. (p. 33)

We are leagues away from doomed ships drifting endlessly under the effect of an unknown curse. The ghost of Coleridge's Ancient Mariner has been exorcised. And when the ship sinks at last, its motto, the epitome of Victorianism, vanishes also, as do the symbols and emblems of Holy Writ, but we must not forget that the doors of renascence – and of the East – have been thrown wide open.

AN INTOXICATING TALE

Marlow does not pay much attention to the possible connotations of the emblems which he weaves into the pattern of the narrative and seems to take them at face value. That is why we would do well to let him continue on his way and not pay attention to his attempts to explain the meaning of the narrative. The vis comica of Marlow's manias has not gone unnoticed; commentators usually quote them as evidence of Conrad's humour, as, for instance, in the case of the recurring refrain in 'Youth', 'Pass the bottle'. There was really nothing significant about it, they said. Conrad was only adding the finishing touch to round out the character/narrator Marlow. It seems to us, however, that Marlow sees double – sees trouble. 'Pass the bottle' is no mere flourish but something at once more serious and more joyous. Marlow's demand for wine should be placed in a context of allusions and puns made behind his back. The rhetoric of 'Youth' owes some of its unusual flavour to just a little too much wine. Like the coal smouldering in the hold of the ship, the wine casts its light (claret/clarity) on the narrator's words, contributing more than a little to Marlow's rediscovery of the East. Wine is a fitting fuel for his illumination, for his return to the past. Of course, of source, you may be shocked by our interpretation, for there is a consensus concerning Marlow. Critics agree that he is quite respectable, a projection of Conrad himself. We will have to prove that Marlow does not always walk in a straight line and our task will not be made any easier because of his sailor's tendency to take off without warning on a new tack. Marlow asks for the bottle to be passed five times. It is the anonymous narrator who notes that Marlow drinks for the sixth and seventh times: 'He drank . . . He drank again.' We may imagine by this time that Marlow has confiscated the bottle or that his cohorts do not dare retrieve it. Should we be speaking of only one bottle? Such circumstantial evidence, however, is not enough to convict him. A more clinical analysis of Marlow's breath is called for.

It is obvious from the outset that the narration jumps from one subject to another and that its components seem at times to be more or less miraculously transubstantiated – a parody of the Last Supper. Thus when he tells the story of the thirsty crew labouring over their inferno of a ship, Marlow links the episode to his own thirst: 'But generally we were taciturn and serious and thirsty. And we had to be careful with the water. Strict allowance. The ship smoked, the sun blazed . . . Pass the bottle.' (p. 21) Water is being changed into wine before our very eyes and the narrative is still progressing from one parable to another. Curiously enough, some words slip noiselessly into the narrative as if they had sprung spontaneously from the context. Thus a reference is made at one stage to putting a stopper on the fire: '. . . it would put a stopper on the fire'. We cannot rule out the possibility that the bottle has just been snatched successfully away from Marlow and corked up again. Confusion and coincidence are even more striking in other passages. When the ship is repaired after the collision with a steamer, Marlow makes a strange comment. It is as if he only grasps metaphors that are within range of his tongue: 'She was recaulked, new coppered and made as tight as a bottle.' Who is inebriated, the ship or the sailor? At another point in the story, bottle combines with battle to make a fine heroic doublet in the description of the crew assembled around the fire: 'Each man had the marks as of a battle about him . . . and each man had a bottle between his legs.' (p. 33) As a matter of fact, it seems that Mahon proves that his reputation is well deserved in this episode and makes an exemplary display of Mahonliness 'with an uncorked bottle in his hand.' It is Mahon and not the skipper who turns out to be the real leader of the expedition.

The latter, who cannot take spirits, is collapsed in a heap on his sofa. He has a title but no power; he has a beard in name only. At this point the story reaches the limits which set it apart from the tall tale, as Marlow's method of narrating the episode of the rats leaving the ship shows: 'Rat after rat appeared on our rail, took a last look over his shoulder and leaped with a hollow thud into the empty hulk.' (p. 17) Such humorous rats, such sentimental and mawkish rats, seem to spring out of the bottle and its excesses. In spite of Marlow's joyful raving, there is no need to assume that, like Mahon, he is often in an inebriated state. His particular form of intoxication, his particular brand of intoxication, seems to be related to the realisation that he will never again relive his lost youth, that his high hopes and his high spirits are lost for ever. We do not wish to be disrespectful of Marlow but we are forced to take into account the numerous allusions and puns which are based on references to food and drink. Do we need to point out again that as in 'Falk' the story is told around a dinner table? Little trace is left of the meal, but the presence of the bottle of claret and the glasses indicates that the other species for communion, the bread, has been taken away. Indeed, the repast is the framework of the narrative and relates directly to what takes place within the narrative itself. The voyage gets off to an ominous start under the guidance of a pilot who 'dodged all day long about the galley drying his handkerchief before the stove'. He is a domestic pilot whose need for security contrasts with Marlow's thirst for adventure. He is a pilot who never loses sight of land between Newcastle and London – a man whose first consideration is his safety.[1] The galley, however, like the men's sense of security, is soon destined to explode in a kind of Rabelaisian conflagration.

> There was a deck-house forward which contained the galley, the cook's berth and the quarters of of the crew . . . the house was shattered as if a shell had exploded inside. Most of it had gone overboard – stove, men's quarters and their property was all gone. (p. 13)

The only survivor, miraculously preserved in the midst of the debacle, is the cook, whose name, lest we forget, is Abraham, a man who clings body and soul to the *Judea*:

> But two posts, holding a portion of the bulkhead to which Abraham's bunk was attached, remained as if by miracle. We

groped in the ruins and came upon this and there he was sitting in
his bunk surrounded by foam and wreckage, jabbering cheerfully
to himself. He was out of his mind completely and forever mad
with this sudden shock coming upon the fag-end of his endurance.
(p. 13)

The cook's madness and his sudden uselessness seem to be one of the
necessary conditions for the survival of the crew. Abraham may well
cling to his berth, to his birth, but the domestic world which he
looked after has been wrecked. The East can only be reached on the
condition that the Western hearth be destroyed. We should not be
surprised to note that Marlow and the other members of the crew do
not show undue sympathy for the unfortunate keeper of civilisation.
With a brutality reminiscent of the March Hare and the Mad
Hatter squeezing the Dormouse's head into a teapot, Marlow and
the other members of the crew hurl the cook down the ladder and
into the hold with great alacrity: 'We snatched him up, lugged him
aft and pitched him head first down the cabin companion.' The
complete disintegration of domestic values and the final stage of
their deliverance comes with the disappearance of the captain's
table, which vanishes with all the instruments: 'Where we had our
breakfast that morning we saw a great hole in the floor.' A chasm
has opened under the mainstay of civilisation; hell now holds the
deck, and old values are called into question: 'The deck being blown
up, it had fallen down into the lazarette of course.' Thus the belly of
civilisation having exploded, and coal, the fuel of European hearths,
having burnt itself out in an absurd display of fireworks, a new dawn
can rise. Astonishingly enough, the crew is 'making merry amidst
violence and disorder', eating bread and cheese – and drinking
stout. Appetites are quite sharp now, the deck is full of spiritual
savagery of a kind that brings to mind Arthur Rimbaud's poem on
hunger in 'Une Saison en Enfer':

> Mangez les cailloux qu'on brise,
> Les vieilles pierres d'église;
> Les galets des vieux déluges,
> Pains semés dans les vallées grises.[2]

In order to discover the East, it is necessary to go beyond the vale of
tears and drift along with Noah, Noah, who is not ashamed of his
vineyard and will not have it tended to in parable only:

'Everybody was on the broad grin. This was on a Friday.' Friday/
fry day, cannibalism is close at hand – and mouth – on the Christian
day of fast. Out of the ashes of the old order, a new Adam, a bit
battered perhaps, conscious of all his ribs appears, a new man, fresh
from the mould of creation and purged of guilt, who approaches the
gates of the East: 'My face felt raw, every limb ached as if broken
and I was aware of all my ribs and would have sworn to a twist in the
backbone.' ('Youth', p. 31)

It is possible therefore, to come to symbolic terms with Marlow's
inebriation. In this light, the wine has the power of reviving the fire
in his heart which he thought had gone out long ago, and the claret
of the opening scene is more than an image of past carousals. In
other words, for Marlow that bottle could be an antidote to an
existence devoid of flavour which evokes a lingering fiery thirst for
youth and the pure spirit of romance.

SECOND EAST

Reaching the portals of the East in his open boat, with his tongue
parched – 'I remember sixteen hours on end with a mouth as dry as
cinder' – Marlow catches a glimpse of a red light signalling the
entrance to a harbour: 'We had made out the red light in the bay
and steered for it, guessing it must mark some small coasting port'.
The modest signal light comes as something of a disappointment
after the conflagration which had lit up the *Judea* after the
explosion. It seems for all the world as if Marlow's route had taken
him back to his starting point, to the ominous red light of the
steamer which had collided with the *Judea* in Falmouth dock. The
collision had taken place amidst shouts, calls to order and bell-
ringing. The steamer – which ironically enough, had a woman's
name, *Melissa* – and its red light bring to mind unpleasant
associations, but that is not the only reminder of the West which
Marlow encounters. The East welcomes Marlow not only with a
Western light but with a Western voice, with a Falmouth/foul
mouth voice: 'And before I could open my lips, the East spoke to
me, but it was a Western voice.' The East is no longer a world apart.
Westerners have exported their language there and aggressive
words explode like bombshells in the silence; 'The voice swore and
cursed violently; it riddled the solemn peace of the bay by a volley of
abuse. It began by calling me pig.' The complexity of Eastern

riddles has been shed, has been riddled and replaced by the language of the West which puts efficiency first. It is as ironic that this language should be Christian as it is that Christianity should be the civilisation of conquest. When you stop to think about it, however, both language and religion follow in the wake of the will to rule, and the division of the world into two theological and geographical hemispheres is but one more projection of this desire to rule. The voice which hails Marlow comes from on board a steamer called the *Celestial*. (Is any commentary really necessary?) Although he thoroughly loathes that voice, Marlow is unavoidably bound to it. We might even say doubly bound to it, since the crew of the *Judea* will return to England aboard the *Celestial*. As in 'Heart of Darkness' where another Marlow makes an eleventh hour alliance with Kurtz, the Marlow of 'Youth' lowers his flags and resigns himself to return to the fold. The time of revolt is over; his rebellion slowly gives way to submission, to peace with a heavenly power – the *Celestial*! Marlow is an accomplice of the Western conquest. Having reached the limits of a new world, he needs friends to turn to in order to have them share in his conqueror's joy: 'A splashing of oars, a measured dip reverberating on the level of the water, intensified by the silence of the shore into loud claps, made me jump up. A boat, a European boat was coming in.' With words that are less vulgar and less deafening than those of the man from the *Celestial*, Marlow invokes the name of the dead: 'I hailed', "*Judea* ahoy".' It is a somewhat ludicrous call which echoes across the seas like the distress signal sent by Captain Beard from the dock in the heart of the Falmouth night. Doesn't it have domestic overtones? Confronted by a silence which he perceives as ominous and which represents an untapped store of unknown words, Marlow seeks comfort in the brotherhood of language, in the comfort of a sympathetic listener. His submission is in direct relation to the authority of the dominating voice aboard the *Celestial*, however, and demonstrates quite adequately the affinities which the insulting voice of the sailor/soldier and the 'measured voice of the philosopher' have in common.[17] Both are equally self-confident – unjustly so – even if the more liberal and tolerant voice of the philosopher lays claim to more foresight than does the rude voice of the soldier. Marlow is just as much of an accomplice of the conquest as the obscene sailor is. His complicity is not only that of the young Marine officer on the road to promotion, but also that of the narrator who makes use of the knowledge which he has in common with his audience. Marlow's story, which echoes the conquest, is by no means an innocent one; the philosopher follows in the steps of the soldier. In telling the story of his first adventure – for the hundredth time, no doubt – Marlow pleads for the legitimacy of the quest and the righteousness of Western civilisation. He is trying to write his own version of history. Like Livius and Virgil who described the founding of their city and of their Empire, Marlow is both historian and spokesman for the British Empire. It is relevant that his audience, a triumvirate composed of pillars of the Empire, are respectively a lawyer, an accountant and a company director, whose functions Marlow does not question and which his story will justify. In this light, we can measure all the ramifications of the irony which wills that Marlow should be welcomed to the East by the booming, warlike voice from the *Celestial*, by the voice of military colonial conquest, by the voice of one of Kipling's soldiers. The scribe, as usual, is not in the forefront of the conquest but is obliged to follow along behind. But like an old soldier remembering past glory, Marlow sings the *res gestae* of the Empire in a voice that is practically overwhelmed by nostalgia and sentiment: 'Ah the good old times – the good old times!' His voice, full of tears and sighs, is not unlike that of the tortoise in *Alice in Wonderland* who also regrets the good old days. It is on purpose that Marlow gives only a vague image of the East. He wants the goal of the romantic quest to be as misty and indefinite as possible in order to make it more attractive to young heroes setting out. That is why it is indispensable for him to give the Orient an enigmatic and eerie character. Even the people of the East described by Marlow in 'Youth' have no real substance. They are seen only obliquely or indirectly, like reflections on the sea which a light gust of wind can ripple and distort like some frail fresco:

> I sat up suddenly. A wave of movement passed through the crowd from end to end, passed among the heads, swayed the bodies, ran along the jetty like a ripple on the water, like a breath of wind on a field – and all was still again. ('Youth', p. 41)

If Marlow lowers his voice with respect, it is only because he is approaching the sanctuary of the story, the secret cell where the alchemists' stone glows like a diamond in its setting of words. Beware of Marlow. True silence is not found, as he claims, at the end of the journey. He skilfully diverts the attention of the audience to the external aspects of the narrative, to the eternal Orient on the horizon, but we should not be duped. The external side of the story, of history, will ensure the development of quest and conquest, but we must refuse to be taken in by Marlow's pseudo-philosophical silence, which has nothing at all to do with philosophy. Marlow's silence, which Western critics have been so eager to praise as full of hidden, transcendantal meaning, is really the silence of someone who is at a loss for words and does not really know what to say next. The ironic silence – of the author, not Marlow – lies in the deepest recess of the text which deceives both eye and ear. That silence points out the false nature of the seemingly triumphant rhetoric of Marlow. Marlow is not aware that his voice is echoing strangely, that it is not ringing true. We have already mentioned the network of allusions to inebriety, but the allusions to lost youth are just as important:

> Her youth was where mine is – where yours is – you fellows who listen to this yarn; and what friend would throw your years and your weariness in your face? (p. 17)

We should watch with our ears/years and listen with our eyes (weary/wary) in order not to fall victim to the siren's voice which Marlow uses to seduce and fool his listeners. We should look for the patterns like the mahogany table at which Marlow and his friends are seated, whose surface, like the sea itself, reflects the bottle, the glasses, and the faces of men who are no longer young: 'I see a bay, a wide bay, smooth as a glass and polished like ice, shimmering in the dark.' With Marlow's hail to the *Celestial*, the surface of the table and the surface of the sea come together. Not only patterns but nouns also, should be carefully examined in a text like 'Youth'. Cònrad was fond of praising Cunninghame Graham for his enigmatic manner of writing 'à mots couverts'[4] for art, like the telling of tales, erases old surfaces so as to paint them anew. Just as Captain Beard tries to make his boat as good as new, just as he has the old motto 'Do or Die' given a new coat of paint, so are old arks or archetypes made to pass for new ones in the story. We should not believe in Marlow's version of history. He is restoring and regilding the blazon of the Empire – of the old Christian civilisation – before sending it out to sea again. Across a nostalgic sea salted with his own tears, the old follower of the sea rows the imperial galley, which admittedly, is not that young any more but which can still make a glorious blaze before disappearing. Galley is an unpleasant word suggesting torture and slavery but it also refers directly to books and printing. What Marlow tries to pass off on us is a recaulked, re-corded, recooked version of a left-over colonial adventure. We should not be deceived by that misty-eyed romantic vision. 'Youth' is an intoxicating narrative in more than one sense. Marlow's after-dinner rhetoric should not prevent us from realising that Conrad sets out to cast doubts upon a certain official version of history and to destroy the romantic myth of the enigmatic East. Both the teller and the tale seem to be under the influence of intoxicating spirits; the *Judea* seems to pitch and roll like the imbiber who tries to hide his lurching gait in mists of volubility.

3 The Enclosure of Death

In the immensity is a beach, a fragile stretch of sand separating the impenetrability of the tropical forest from the endless blue ocean:

We landed on a bit of white beach. It was backed by a low cliff wooded on the brow, draped in creepers to the very foot. Below us the plain of the sea, of a serene and intense blue, stretched with a slight upward tilt to the thread-like horizon drawn at the height of our eyes. Great waves of glitter blew lightly along the pitted dark surface, as swift as feathers chased by the breeze. A chain of islands sat broken and massive facing the wide estuary, displayed in a sheet of pale and glassy water reflecting faithfully the contour of the shore. High in the colourless sunshine a solitary bird, all black, hovered, dropping and soaring above the same spot with a slight rocking motion of the wings. A ragged, sooty bunch of flimsy mat hovels was perched over its own inverted image upon a crooked multitude of high piles the colour of ebony. (*Lord Jim*, p. 244).

In this passage, space and time no longer exist, the narration is suspended, and the writing manages to capture the awesome quality of the fleeting moment. The setting, which seems almost illusory and unreal, reflects admirably the ephemeral aspect of *Lord Jim*, a book where everything – or nothing – is possible. The beach is a frontier which is subjected to the combined pressure of the primeval forest and of the open sea. Because of the double danger of being overrun by the creeping vegetation or of being carried out to sea by the tides, it maintains its precarious balance with difficulty – like Lord Jim does. It is the last leg of a journey into the heart of darkness, a last reprieve before going upstream to put one's idea of honour to the test:

but it seems to me that for each of us going home must be like going to render an account. We return to face our superiors, our

23

kindred, our friends – those whom we obey and those whom we love. (p. 162)

In *Lord Jim* space and time are used to create a new fictional universe. Unlike the setting of Conrad's earlier novels – closed and decaying worlds – this one is put into historic and geographical perspectives which, strangely enough seems to ensure a higher degree of inviolability and integrity. This change of perspective is intrinsic to the development of the story as a whole. Instead of being portrayed in the sphere he has always known, the hero is sent to a new one where his role will be that of reagent or regenerator.

Patusan, where Jim lands in search of personal rehabilitation, shelters hostile camps of Arabs and Malays separated by a river. If one is to believe the portrait which Marlow gives of him, Raja Tunku Allang, the Sultan's uncle, is a truly degenerate figure. Muslim vigour and rigour are represented by Sherif Ali, a religious warrior and leader of the inland tribes, whom Jim, as a representative of imperial Britain, will expel from his stronghold – just the reverse of Gordon's saga. We must not forget, however, that Sherif Ali, who is called a 'half-bred' and a 'wandering stranger', does not have a legitimate, hereditary claim to the land. The other ethnological presence in Patusan, sixty Bugi families, members of a Malay tribe, owe allegiance to Doramin, a patriarch mellowed by the presence of his wife. These immigrants from the Celebes have no more claim than do the Muslims to the region of Patusan. It is their superior intelligence, sharpened in conflicts with their Muslim rivals, which gives the Malays their advantage. Moreover, in his son Dain Waris, Doramin has the hope of founding a dynasty that will put an end to the political instability in the country. Jim is a new variation on an old theme. The passive Almayer and the dissolute Willems epitomised the failure of the White adventure. In their helplessness, they implicated Lingard, their father and benefactor, in grotesque rescue operations. In Conrad's first novels, it was the necessity of the intrigue which dictated the movement of the characters towards failure; with *Lord Jim*, the end result is the same but the hero, instead of remaining outside the native sphere of things and submitting to his fate in splendid isolation, causes the ruin of the local community. Doramin, the Bugi patriarch, loses his son because of Jim's blundering efforts to ensure continuity and tradition.

Marlow, who in the circumstance is a father figure like Lingard, is categoric about the achievement of his protégé: 'My last words about Jim shall be few. I affirm he had achieved greatness.' (p. 165) Because he believes in Jim's greatness Marlow implicitly condones his heroic ideal. Yet his approbation should not be taken out of context but must be considered in the perspective of the complex narration which Conrad develops. Without belittling the unique poetry which characterises the novel, we must take into account that Marlow's democratic attachment to Jim makes him blind to some of his more obvious failings. It is the complexity of the narration itself, and the diverse perspectives which it opens, which allow the reader to make his own judgements. We must always bear in mind that Marlow, however attractive his point of view may be and no matter how poetically expressed, is a hagiographer writing the life of a 'saint'. And if we stop and think about it, isn't Kurtz presented in much the same manner in 'Heart of Darkness'?

In comparison with the grotesque adventures against which it is measured in the novel, Jim's romantic quest in the closed world of Patusan has many of the attributes of a chivalric initiation rite. On a personal level, Jim undoubtedly achieves greatness. His personal refusal to make compromises and his desire for independence compel our admiration all the more because, as he roams the South Seas, he comes up against an anonymous gang of derelicts and drifters. And yet, Jim's heroism, pushed to its absolute limits, is defined negatively – we only know what he is not – in relation to similar quests which surround his own. His solitude is threatened everywhere in the book by parodic mimetism and the presence of doubles, couples and crowds whom he loathes beyond the shadow of his guilt. Thus the appearance of a group of Cook & Sons tourists has the effect of making him silent and angry. Marlow, his confessor, must take great pains to make him break his silence. The social amenity of a little wine – a comic stratagem worthy of the plump, easy-going Sancho that Marlow is – only produces an outburst of pathos which shocks the globe-trotters having lunch at a near-by table. Threatened by counterfeits and imitations, Jim's original heroic pattern requires protection and isolation in order to survive. Hence the joint decision taken by Stein and Marlow to send him to the safety of Patusan where his genuine double, ironically enough, will seek him out and challenge him. Gentleman Brown, who makes the same claim to being evil as Jim does to being good, intrudes on the isolation of Patusan, on the mysterious island, on the kind of Treasure Island where two ageing adolescents, Marlow and Stein, have intended, through Jim, to restore their faith in their own devalued dreams.

Marlow speaks highly of Jim's purity and claims that it is a 'faith mightier than the laws of order and progress', but nowhere does he define it. The naïve reader is left, like the privileged listener who acts as Marlow's sounding board from somewhere deep within the text – but how deep? – with the task of defining this colonial purity without trespassing beyond the limits that fiction has carefully laid out – at the risk of passing quite innocently, like Jim himself, through the looking-glass, into an imaginary world. Yet we know from the outset what Jim's colonial purity is not. It is not the re-edition of long-finished eighteenth-century explorations whose deformed version is found in Robinson and Chester, the abominable 'cannibal' of the Southern Seas and his Australian partner, whose investment in guano, a faecal ersatz of fabulous visions of gold, vanishes like a child's bubble somewhere off Walpole Reef.[1] Nor is it the methodical (or Methodist, perhaps?), sordid adventure of Gentleman Brown, a romantic rebel to the last, even to the portals of death, a bloodthirsty pirate with repressed religious longings, whose finest hour came when he seduced the wife of a missionary sent to Melanesia to convert unbelievers. Nor is it the vocation, thwarted by accident, of a pastor leading his spiritual flock to the sanctuaries of Arabia. Without a doubt, Jim's colonial purity is much closer to the primary impulsion described by Marlow as the major reason for the early maritime expansion, a passion for spices setting palates and spirits afire, whose legend is embellished and magnified by the even more demanding tastes of seasoned veterans. Not one of these definitions really applies to Jim – and yet all of them do in a way – for with his fine soul he claims to be above them. Jim represents the supreme development of philosophical exoticism, which can only be perpetuated and survive through the hero's refusal to take on a visible human form. This tenet reveals a great deal about the thought-patterns of the West, where an ideal can only be defined by what it is not. Truth is set up as an ideal to be attained, but it is a fragmented ideal, a messianic ideal to be reached only through complete negation – through death. To bury Jim, to bury him alive, as Marlow's suggests to Stein, echoes Judge Brierly's pessimism:

> I had quoted poor Brierly's remark: 'let him creep twenty feet underground and stay there'. He looked up at me with interested attention, as though I had been a rare insect. 'This could be done,

too' he remarked, sipping his coffee. 'Bury him in some sort' I explained. 'One doesn't like to do it of course, but it would be the best thing seeing what he is.' (p. 161)

Patusan, of course, is perfectly suited to the man who would be a hero. Patusan is like a tomb. Geographically speaking, it is as quiet as a grave because the stream of civilisation, branching east and south-east, bypasses it completely. Practically speaking, it has been a tomb, once before, as we can infer from Marlow's cryptic remark about Stein's method of solving Jim's problem: 'I can only guess that once before Patusan had been used as a grave for some sin, transgression or misfortune.' Then, too, there are the linguistic slips of the master of the brigantine who brings Jim to Patusan, whose comic imitation of the English language only serves to heighten the impact of his words: 'the gentleman was already "in the similitude of a corpse. . . . Already like the body of one deported".' Symbolically speaking, Patusan is a tomb, too, a twilight space whose geographic and cosmic elements seem to suggest the sinister effects of death.[2] Contrary to kindly appearances, the paternal instinct which drives the ageing duo of Marlow and Stein to exclude, to bury, the guilty son, indicates a morbid kinship. Not enough attention has been paid to the desire of Stein and Marlow to bring together fragments of space or to the secret bond which connects the symbolic repartition of space to the Christian economic system. Patusan is a religious tomb, a kind of purgatory where the moral rehabilitation of the hero takes place after his initial confession. Consequently, it is an enchanted place, a mythical enclosure which the chivalric commercial order preserves secretly in order to mend and amend its models and where the bustle of economic activity is brought to a complete standstill – an economic miracle of negativity. Patusan – Avalon – Death. The vertical immobility of the forest contrasts with the horizontal drifting motion of the wanderers. Space in Patusan turns around the pivotal figure of Jim, who partakes of the immobility of the spell 'as if under an enchanter's wand', and of the endless immobility of trade: 'No magician's wand can immobilise him under my eyes. He is one of us.' Guided by Marlow's persuasive voice, many critics speak of Jim's capricious and unfathomable liberty. Would it not be more accurate to speak of a sacrificial offering of the guilty son by the fathers in order to ensure the continuing division of commerce and religion and the justification of Western expansion? The arbitrary power of law, in this instance maritime law, creates guilt and demands suitable punishment for transgressions. In this case the punishment is confinement to land: it is one way of justifying the law and the fundamental injustice of the judicial system. In other words, the rigid structure of the Christian economic system needs to be bolstered up by a system of romantic retribution in a kind of wonderland, on a kind of enchanted island where the law can assume a variety of disguises and where children like Lord Jim can pretend to be heroes:

> The conquest of love, honour, men's confidence – the pride of it, the power of it, are fit material for a heroic tale; only our minds are struck by the externals of such a success, and to Jim's successes there were no externals. (p. 166)

And now that we have drawn the symbolic map of Patusan which is used as a reservation where innocence can be restored – reclaimed – we must speak of death and time in their relation to romance. In *Lord Jim* there is an almost obsessive preoccupation with them, which takes on a variety of technical and symbolic forms. If we consider the drama alone, that is to say only the intrigue of the story, time, although it includes both ruptures and pauses, appears none the less to be linear and continuous. There is the unending and harmonious vision of time on board the *Patna* where the cosmic, psychological, and mechanical rhythms are unified in a single sphere. There is the reiterative time of anamnesis when guilt is analysed, there is the confessional exchange between Marlow and Jim when Marlow prepares Jim's redemption. There is romantic time which seems to expand infinitely, where the genealogy of the action is enriched by the use of many diverse legends. These three conceptions of time are the source of the three main rhythmic divisions of the drama and they are held together by transitory rhythms springing either from the more relaxed mode of comedy (the episodes with the crew of the *Patna* or Jim's departure for Patusan on board the brigantine) or from a more concentrated symbolic mode (the episode of the New England alarm clock, that Puritan mechanism, which wakens Jim and sends him into the world of 'romance', thus erasing the memory of his first guilty leap). The profound originality of the book lies in its alternation of rhythms and tempos which are chosen to suit different, even contradictory genres.[3]

Now, what we should consider the most important aspect of *Lord Jim*, even if it is not perfectly evident at first, and even if it has not attracted much serious critical attention, is the manner in which the different episodes are held together. The intrigue of *Lord Jim*, whose apparent continuity is made up of ruptures and reversals, takes second place to the narration as a whole, which appears to recede before it. This is the nature of Conrad's most original innovation and of his greatest novelty. Like his hero, he makes a qualitative leap which takes him from the realistic portrayal of a world like Berau to the ambiguous portrayal of a world like Patusan. Tested first in the Orient, in Patusan, his new approach to the composition – and the decomposition – of the fictional material will be used successively in Africa, London, South America and Geneva. Conrad works ceaselessly to refine his technique and the questions asked in each successive book will become more and more pertinent.

Marlow's manner of narrating the story in *Lord Jim* should be considered as an important technical innovation. It is different from the method used in 'Youth' and 'Heart of Darkness' in so far as the irony of the text as a whole does not appear to be directly submitted to the control of the author. In other words, the relationship of the narrator and the hero in *Lord Jim* is not put into perspective for the reader by the discreet intervention of a third person, the author. As a result of this the narration takes on a kind of mythical status rarely taken into account by critics.[4] In successfully putting together and giving coherence to Jim's biography, Marlow needs to be as persevering as a private eye (in Raymond Chandler's books, one of his literary descendants will actually become a private investigator) and as understanding as a confessor. As a matter of fact, if Marlow did not tell us that 'a confounded democratic quality or vision' counselled him to help Jim, we might well wonder what deep human urge was behind his devotion. Marlow's Socratic curiosity and Christian compassion are justification enough from an ethical point of view, of course, but these human motives should not make us forget that as narrator he often presents Jim's case in a light best suited to his own purposes or that, at times, the story escapes his control, bound up as it is with what he calls fate, or destiny, which have their source in myth.

'*In articulo mortis.*' In order to sound the depths of the matter, we must see Marlow as he really is and not only as the compassionate protector of Jim. Marlow is a narrator, a creator who brings forth characters in a trice, at the splice of a yard, at the spin of a yarn – a man dealing daily in life and death. Symbolically and thematically speaking, *Lord Jim* is everywhere littered with fragments of human lives and pieces of human wreckage. *Lord Jim* is a prophetic novel in the sense that it reveals for the first time in Conrad's writing an abstract conception of time and space, composed equally of fragmentation and continuity, which will eventually become the hallmark of his work. Ever since its beginnings in the eighteenth century, the novel had aimed at biographical exhaustivity. This intention persists in *Lord Jim*. Marlow, the mender of fates, pieces together bits of information, and it is his smooth, flowing voice which holds everything together. In its abundant use of detail, the narration seems to complete with the precision of the civil registry and appears to be an exhumation of dead souls or a compilation of last wishes. Prisoners of their guano reefs given new life by the power of legends, the characters stand out as more or less isolated concentric islands, each one surrounded by the deep fault of death, a break in the landscape that the sea soothes like a balm. Assuming the mask of an eternal wanderer on that sea, Marlow circulates among the various solidified fragments of land like a kind of Ulysses who has somehow managed to escape the lure of the isles. Because of the mask which he wears, time in the narrative passages appears to be as endless and as innocent as the meanderings of Marlow, appears to be without beginning and without end, to be cosmic, like the rhythm of the sea and the movement of the planets. Marlow's fate is to have the gift of relating events but not to have complete control over the meaning which will be given to his words. Most often, in his search for significant expression, he chooses an image taken from the cosmos where the planets, fellow prisoners of time and space, are harnessed under the double yoke of simultaneity and excentricity.[5]

In the practice of his art, which is at once both anonymous and immortal, Marlow becomes a fisher of men. He alone among the teeming masses of characters in the novel manages to escape death. Even the privileged listener, the supreme narrator of the tale, feels, in the prison of his study,[6] its menacing, oppressive presence. Space is divided and fragmented down to the very last detail of the text. Even Marlow's narration ends in fragments – in the series of letters which he sends posthumously, seemingly in order to escape the funeral oration, in order to avoid telling of Jim's death and more important, to escape from the very mention of death. He leaves to the privileged listener the task of assembling the patchwork pattern of fragmented truth. *Lord Jim* makes its way through a series of fractures and ruptures which have been cleverly mended, but we should ask ourselves whether this apparent progression does not in fact mask a real regression. Does not the story implicitly criticise the distribution of space in the temporal order of things? The narration is not content with reproducing, biographically, the frailties of men in order to find a cure for them, but sets out to provoke their stumbles. The narration seems to thrive on catastrophe and to enjoy toying with the here and the hereafter of death.

What are we to conclude about death and the relation of romance to death? What exactly is the sacrificial power of writing? What are we to think about the initial violence which erupts and fragments space in order to make it conform to a time sequence? By locking Jim up or, more literally, by burying him alive in the confined area of Patusan, does not the narration expose – even over-expose – the arbitrariness of the law and of the genealogical order? In the heroic and anti-heroic genealogy of the book (oh, ironic transmission!) a series of deaths – those of the *Patna*'s engineer, of Brierly, Dain Waris and Gentleman Brown – precede Jim's for the very reason that their blood is necessary for the consecration of the romantic altar and the presentation of the sacrificial offering. Thus, Conrad masks a regression under the appearances of a progression, at least as Marlow tells the story. He makes a case for the legitimacy of the hero through his use of suspense, through his hagiographic presentation, through his quasi-paternal self-effacement in pretending to be lagging behind the son he is preceding.

This is the moment to speak of Marlow's progression towards another prodigal son, toward Kurtz, whose legendary weight (note the inversion of the image . . . Anchises carrying Aeneas) will for ever be a burden for Marlow. A close examination of *Lord Jim* reveals an extensive use of death-oriented economics which is intimately linked to the fulfilment of temporal goals and the negative occupation of space – Patusan is a prime example of this. Similarly, any unexpected expression of profound conviction, like Jim's impulsive and spontaneous romanticism, which fragments and alters language, is relentlessly reintegrated by teachers like Marlow and Stein into the existing universe.[7] The dream of life must be preserved and Jim's outbursts must be codified and given their proper place; that is to say, he must somehow be integrated into the cosmos, if only as a star of the fifth order. Death has an almost mythical power. In the galaxy where Puritan guilt and romantic aspirations meet, a chrysalis has no chance of being metamorphosed into a butterfly. It will be left to another Marlow to discover, almost in spite of himself, far up the Congo river, at an outport of civilisation and at the end of the colonial adventure to what point life and death have been domesticated, have lost their original meaning, in the Western world's attempt to dominate space with its powerful economic system.

Now we can return to the lonely stretch of beach which Marlow glimpses on leaving Patusan before setting out again for the open spaces of the Pacific. The beach is the symbol of a tale whose vistas look out towards infinity. It is essential that the story should leave behind it a petrified fragment of itself, a store of pure matter, a paradigm, a legacy for future generations. Thus the tale has an elliptical form with two focal points, Marlow and Jim. It is only in keeping with the vestal-like figure of Jim,[8] guardian of one of the symbolic hearths, that the narration should have the task of keeping alive the sacred flame, of seeing to it that the infiniteness of the universe is preserved and that no power is allowed to dominate its vast space. Thus the tale, like a window opening on the ocean, lets in the invigorating sea air which is essential to the life of the narrator and of the story:

> till suddenly at a bend it was as if a great hand far away had lifted a heavy curtain, had flung open an immense portal. The light itself seemed to stir, the sky above our heads widened, a far off murmur reached our ears, a freshness enveloped us, filled our lungs, quickened our thoughts, our blood, our regrets – and straight ahead, the forest sank down against the dark-blue ridge of the sea.
>
> I breathed deeply, I revelled in the vastness of the opened horizon, in the different atmosphere that seemed to vibrate with the toil of life, with the energy of an impeccable world. This sky and this sea were open to me. The girl was right – there was a sign, a call in them – something to which I responded with every fibre of my being. I let my eyes roam through space, like a man released from bonds who stretches his cramped limbs, runs, leaps, responds to the inspiring elation of freedom. (p. 244)

The life breath of the story and its central image. Would Marlow object if we looked ahead to the Sulaco mine or to the icy waters of Lake Leman? What is revealed for the first time in the subterranean landscape of *Lord Jim* is the presence of a fault, a kind of continental divide that begins with this novel and runs all across Conrad's major work. Fault, why not fatality? The fatality of the temporal order of things, which is only constituted and perpetuated by the refinement with which time-frames are endlessly fashioned and their sequences varied – the economics of exploiting mineral substance being closely linked to the aesthetics of representative art. Thus the succession of images and the inversion of their chronological order are destined to make the tale blind to its own impact. The tale is like a monster with an insatiable appetite for biographies which end in death. Right from the beginning, it is an exotic, exautic monster. If *Lord Jim* is successful as a novel, it is because Conrad seems to have struck a balance between the demands of intrigue and the demands of symbolic imagery and myth. In *Lord Jim* Conrad is equally distant from perfect unity and absolute fragmentation, from immortality and death. A beach? A borderline?

Part II
The Colonial Imposture

4 Deviations

. . . we knew we were fated, before the ebb began to run, to hear about one of Marlow's inconclusive experiences.

'Heart of Darkness', p. 51

Cervantes suggests many things but never infers anything.

The Canon, *Don Quixote*

Don Quixote is invulnerable. His paper armour has only one defect, but it is a major one – blows go right through it! This might lead you to believe, of course, that this armour gives him no protection at all, but by placing himself behind the cover of a book, Don Quixote has chosen the best possible hiding place, the most impregnable one for a hero. What does it matter if he is exposed to the dangers of a hostile reality? Because he wears the livery of the written word, he has nothing to fear. Certainly, the books which defend Don Quixote and which he defends – those written for patrons of the arts – are old fashioned ones; their jackets, like his livery, are rumpled and worn. But what better camouflage could be found? This wizard book of spells is only theatre make-up, which hides the amazing youth and agility of the hero. The division, the central fault which differentiates Don Quixote from Sancho Panza, fiction from reality, chivalry from what is common, is apparently the result of the printer's manner of folding the pages. In a humanist era, the pages of a book have to be folded, binding together contrary ideas out of tolerance, and allowing printing on both sides of a page. At the time of Cervantes, however, prudence was the order of the day.[1] That is why it was far better to construct a hero out of a surplus of paper, to speak of Rosinante, an old worn-out hack who appeared in unsold books left on the shelf, in order to preserve the manuscript from the fires of the Inquisition. It was better to create a hero from another time and from another world whose marginal existence would assure the survival of the work, to create a hero too unimportant for burning, a ridiculous heretic, worth no more than a single log and certainly not the number needed to burn him at the stake. Thus Don

Quixote seems to be a figure of pomp and circumstance, a creature of fantasy whose disguise allows him to hide the real meaning of the book up the sleeve of his extravagant costume – the humanist to pass for a monk. Don Quixote is a Utopian figure composed of all the follies and whose follies are blended into one supreme Utopia – the work of art.

In 'Heart of Darkness', Marlow is not a figure made of papier-mâché. The only book which obtains approval in his eyes, the navigation manual which he discovers by chance during his peregrinations, is a model of practicality, a profound treatise which absorbs him only temporarily.

Marlow is not the kind of man to stay sheltered for long – out of the mainstream, so to speak – behind the pages of a book. He has no time to give to them. This rapid passage in front of the mirror, this brief verification of his reflection, only confirms him in his determination to carry out the task at hand and to continue in the direction he had previously chosen. The mirror sends him back to the real world. On the other hand, all the unlikely specimens of humanity whom he encounters in the jungle are flimsy, unreal creatures, like the accountant absorbed in his reckonings or the young Belgian agent who is described as a kind of paper-tiger Mephistopheles. Without his impertinence, Marlow would bear a strong resemblance to Alice in Wonderland, but a grown-up Alice visiting a land of horrors, who would see through the juvenile card game immediately. Or why not Sancho Panza? Cervantes, in-augurating the age of the printed word, created a knight not in shining armour, but in invulnerable paper. Having but little faith in books and Western culture, Conrad roots his helpless knight to the spot and it is the donkey boy who advances. Certainly, donkeys are the favourite mounts of the braggarts who are colonising Africa in 'Heart of Darkness'. At the helm of his steamer, huffing and puffing its way up the river, Marlow, a kind of distrustful and narrow-minded Sancho Panza, navigates by dead reckoning, and unknown to himself, goes to the rescue of his Don Quixote who is prisoner of the bush much as he would be of an enchanted castle. In spite of the fragile nature of his constitution, Don Quixote always knew where he wanted to go. And if he received wounds and hard knocks, it all happened according to the chivalric code. In 'Heart of Darkness', the knight arriving at the end of his quest, where there are no more adventures in store for him, can neither advance nor retreat. Hence the necessity of the expedition of the faithful squire Sancho/

Marlow. After all, it is a classic episode drawn from the adventures of chivalry, somewhat like Richard the Lion Heart waiting for Ivanhoe to come and rescue him, with the difference that, here, the route which leads to the point of rescue is strewn with snares and traps. Don Quixote brandishes his spear according to his whims and enters into a series of helter-skelter adventures which belie the order he dreams of imposing. A very unmethodical individual who accepts no other authority than his own, he could never presume to master the refractory nature of reality.[2] From this point of view, Don Quixote is the model of the hero whose fine soul is not made for this world. In 'Heart of Darkness', on the contrary, the reality of colonialism has its own aristocratic structure. By going up the Congo river, Marlow follows without realising it the itinerary of a medieval quest. All the traditional signs, all the symbolic landmarks appear along his route – but they have been tampered with. Instead of helping him on his way, they mislead him. The blunt spears, the useless books, and the savage round tables have all lost their original meaning; not one of them is what it seems to be, and the conventions of the chivalric code are not respected. Marlow tells us as much in his naïve way, but what he does not know is that the signs are following him and waiting in ambush for him, and that from the heart of the forest Kurtz/Don Quixote is already spinning a web to snare him. Relying on his common sense and placing his trust in his conception of reality, Marlow falls into the trap like any unsuspecting fool. With his head lowered, still believing that books are just not important, and having missed the true sense of the warning constituted by the navigation manual, he will become a hostage, the guardian of the letters which Kurtz/Don Quixote is returning to Dulcinea. Sancho Panza used to rescue his master on occasion. Marlow finds himself a prisoner of 'his master', a prisoner of a papier-mâché figure and of a book, whose misleading character he recognises only in retrospect.

MAPS

Maps do not appear in medieval romances. The quest is a ritual which covers a symbolic territory. Certainly, the succession of forests, clearings, and castles which reoccur constantly, creates an imaginary setting which reflects fairly accurately the real world of feudal Christianity,[3] but it is less a question of topography than of general categories. In the thirteenth century, the Bible was still the foremost authority when it came to geography. In the Bible, the earth appears at the crossroads of Heaven and Earth. Jerusalem, the forbidden and coveted city, reigns at the centre of the world. At the heart of this continuity, however, the appearance of the romance announces a break – the end of a tradition. Every morning the monotony of the horizon is called into question again. In the social order which swings between 'the closed horizons of the clearing' to 'the immense horizons of Christianity where one can go from England to Saint Jacques de Compostelle or to Toledo for Arab culture as do the twelfth century English clerics', the heroic knights dream of faraway places, of somewhere else, of an opening in the world where the first rays of light from the East, the Holy Grail, may be seen. In the place of this vague and indefinite geography, the Renaissance will substitute scientifically defined contours as the need for defined space perceived in the heart of medieval Christianity becomes more pronounced. Maps are drawn up in enclosed places by cartographers. For this reason, fantasy disappears. Elves and monsters, Ariel and Caliban seek refuge on the receding frontiers of the Western world. Shakespeare tries to find correspondences between the map of West Indies and the map of the pathways to the heart. In order to restore the age of romance (*Brave New World*), Prospero agrees to come down from his tower and to break his humanist magician's wand. In the nineteenth century, as the result of a strange alliance, fantasy is united with science. All the literature of adventure – on land and on sea – makes copious use of maps. Stevenson, Rider Haggard, and Jules Verne establish their stories firmly in geography, in the concrete world of real things. When Joseph Conrad begins to write, it is too late; the last phase of dividing up the world has already ended. That is why all his works reflect this ultimate contraction of space and why their tone is one of regret for lost horizons. In 'Heart of Darkness', maps appear at the outset. Is it not Africa itself which looms behind the title and for which the title is a metaphor, a heart and a story which are beating to the rhythm of muffled drums? It is the Africa which has kept the rhythm of primitive times, and the echoes reverberate throughout the story. It is also the Africa whose exploration had hardly begun before the European powers were dividing it up avidly, selling the skin of the lion they had not yet killed. (Remember the Berlin Conference of 1885 during which the fate of the Congo, among other problems, was decided.) The passion for maps of the young

Marlow, and of the young Conrad, is expressed at the beginning of the book: 'Now, when I was a little chap I had a passion for maps.' What attracts Marlow are the white spaces on the maps. White is the colour of the unknown, a dazzling, vague colour, but it is also the symbol of heroism and purity; white like the armour of Galahad, the epitome of knighthood, the purest of the knights who sought the Holy Grail. At this point the irony of Conrad intervenes: for Marlow, the most attractive kind of whiteness is that of the polar regions: 'Certainly, I have never gone there and I never will try again now.'

If he cannot have the whiteness of the Pole, however, Marlow will be content with the whiteness of Africa, 'the biggest and the most blank, so to speak', the whiteness of the second choice, relatively white, which means to say already grey, inasmuch as it is certainly true that Marlow has difficulty not colouring the story with his own disillusionment: 'But there was in it one river especially, a mighty big river . . . And as I looked at the map of it in a shop-window, it fascinated me as a snake would a bird.' Desire and curiosity are represented on this geographical map where the Congo winds along. This fabulous river discovered by chance and almost in a state of delirium by Livingstone, later explored by Stanley, slithers its way across the map and takes on a symbolic value. The Congo is moving; it has a life of its own; it is metamorphosed into that famous figure of the bestiary, serpent of Genesis. We are returning to the source of human existence, to a time when reality was more important than fiction, when Africa lost its status of monster in order to take its place in the geographical system of things. And at that precise moment, Conrad decides to free the African continent from geographical strictures and return it to its original mysterious origins. Paradoxically, in 'Heart of Darkness', we are closer to medieval romance than to the detailed geographical adventure of Victorian times.

Indeed, Conrad projects the real map of Africa on a symbolic plane. In order to do so, he erases all its contours and recognisable places. The most we know is that the river is the Congo, but we cannot identify the different outposts which mark Marlow's way. The names, the only geographical indications we have, all sound alike, as Marlow warns us at the beginning. Thrown up at random on the coast between customs agents and police, they are either lost in the vast landscape or rebound, grotesque and flat-sounding phonemes, against the silent wall of the forest. The mundane approach of the anthropologist, seeking what is real, contrasts with the notion of what is marvellous, realistically so, that one finds in the stories of the Victorian era. The typical image is of a straight and monotonous coast, which is Marlow's despair. As for the symbolism, it is varied, composed of equal measures of Christianity and ancient mythology. The Congo, the serpent of Genesis which fascinated the young Marlow in the shop window in London, is transformed, on the spot, into the river of Hades, Acheron, river of the dead, with its tributary Cocytus, the river of wailing. And it is the Victorian adventure, itself the inheritor of the adventures of the Renaissance, which brings us back to the frontiers of the Middle Ages, to the shadow of Dante's forest (*silva oscura*) where Marlow goes forth (*nel mezzo del cammin*).

This map of Africa is not only turned upside-down and inside-out, however. It is almost as imprecise as the map of medieval romance with its symbolic topography: the forest becoming the equatorial jungle, the clearing the trading posts, and the castles the fortified strongholds. By means of this ironic projection, of this conversion which corresponds to mythology, we are in effect sent back to an unknown continent whose map has not even been sketched yet. White map or black map, the right side or the wrong side, the piece of a game whose outcome has been decided beforehand, the maps of romance have the aspect of a game played in company, in distinguished company, if you wish, of a game which could be played at a Round Table. In the game being played, the rules permit only a limited number of conventions and combinations, but the possibility of beginning the game again as often as one wishes is unlimited. And the Grail is ever present. It is a question of making a king, of holding the winning hand. The tentatives are as numerous as the temptations. In a Victorian adventure, as we have seen, space does not allow you to keep going round and round. From now on, the quest will be linear and will mean going from one place which is known to another which is unknown, so as to be able to map it accurately. It is no longer the game of the quest but of the conquest. Ciphers which hide the mysterious place, like the beetle in 'The Gold Bug' of Edgar Alan Poe, or the cross in Stevenson's *Treasure Island* or the text in a foreign or ancient tongue in Rider Haggard's *She*, uncharted space in Jules Verne's *The Mysterious Island* must all be made intelligible eventually, although it does require a certain openness of mind. Even Phileas Fogg, the prototype of the modern tourist who circles the globe with ease, circumscribing it to verify its boundaries, still has the keys to a game – Passepartout. The game has been scaled down radically; it has become less and less of an adventure. Ironically enough, the missing adventure is compensated for by domesticity itself. Phileas Fogg goes around the world, but he forgets to turn off the gas before leaving. To put things clearly, there will always be a small flame to put out or a gas pilot which needs to be turned up again.[4] With Joseph Conrad, there will be no more games and no more playing. Space has been contracted to the size of a title, of a heart, of an inside-out map. It is no longer a question of the heart of the darkness but of the darkness of the heart. The game is no longer worth playing. In other words, this whole long adventure in space and through space is no longer valid. There will no longer be white against black, Galahad against the wicked knights. White and black are associated indissolubly. In order to come to this, was this long chain of desires and were these lights on the plain disguised as torches of progress, 'running blaze', really necessary? Because, from the very beginning, you see, the outcome was a foregone conclusion: 'We live in a glimmer of light.'

THE BOOK

At the beginning of the medieval quest is the book. Although it is not physically present, it can be found everywhere. Born of themes scattered throughout the original text (like the lance of Longinus or the vase of Joseph of Arimathea), which have been taken out and interwoven in a new pattern, the legend of the Holy Grail rewrites the Book and at the same time indicates the vanity of such an imitation. Retaining its outlines, conferring upon it the finest treasures of language but revealing by the very multitude of descriptions, its unfathomable nature, the legend creates a subtle play of mystery made of both veilings and unveilings.[5] In addition to these numerous but silent appearances, the text also delegates its voice to certain characters such as monks, abbots, wise men and doctors considering marvellous dreams which have been told to them by naïve knights.[6] Writing appears as a sign only from time to time and is only of secondary importance. Most often, it takes the form of unreadable messages such as the one Lavncelot is unable to decipher because night is falling at the entrance to the chapel '*gaste et decheue*'.[7] Profane and illusory writing. It would seem that only one text,

Sacred Writing, that is approached by means of marginal notes and commentaries which read like novels, can exist. Any other graphic presence indicates fraudulent imitation. In Romantic literature as well writing is very often at the origin of the quest. Unless it appears, ironically, at the end, as in the form of mysterious letters, like the ones Gordon Pym finds during the last leg of his journey.

In the Victorian adventure *par excellence*, Rider Haggard's *She*, fragments of slate-bearing Greek inscriptions set the story in motion. These new conventions coincide with the development of the sciences of archeology and philology as well as the beginning of the reign of the written word, which is no longer sacred but profane, which can be understood and translated. There is a new dimension in 'Heart of Darkness'; we no longer encounter fragments of texts but rather an entire book is found along the road of the quest. Having left the Inner Station, Marlow and the pilgrims discover at a bend in the river a hut of reeds (note the type of material – reed – papyrus). Of this discovery, superficial criticism has often retained only one element, the book itself. Without going any farther than its title, *An inquiry into Some Points of Seamanship*, and reasoning by analogy, the conclusion is reached that all the wisdom of Marlow/ Conrad is contained in the volume. We must be on our guard, however, for the text, like the road which leads to Kurtz, is full of traps for the unwary. Before trying to learn why the book is found at this precise location, we must take pains to reflect on the context in which it is found. First of all, this hut has a flag, like any colonial outpost worth the name, but with a difference none the less. This flag flies badly. It is an unglorious and faded replica of the ones which Marlow saw along the coast and which, even then, although the French colours are known for their brilliance, were menaced by the surrounding greyness. This flag has been torn to pieces; it is a flag with no apparent nationality, which is the worst fate that can befall a flag. A neutral insignia, symbol of a meaningless nationalism, it flies at the end of a pole which is ready to fall down: 'an inclined and melancholy pole'. But next to the useless flag, an image of the menaced text, we find a pile of neatly stacked wood which enables Marlow to continue his quest and which gives the text a margin of security – a welcome source of energy. The quest is really a series of relays like the ones found in the adventures of Phileas Fogg, where vehicles are especially important. In this case, however, the story depends on fuel. The juxtaposition of the worn flag and the carefully stacked woodpile are in the image of the different colonial powers.

On the one hand, the vain French conquest in the tradition of Savorgnan de Brazza, which cannot resist the march of time. On the other hand, the less openly chauvinistic and nationalistic one made by the English, certainly more technical, and which was limited for a long time in Africa to trading-posts and warehouses.

But we are still a long way from the book. Several discoveries separate us from it. First of all, there is a plank on the woodpile – wood on wood, book on book, a pencilled sign with a telegraphic message: 'Wood for you. Hurry up. Approach cautiously'. We need to appreciate the true value of the message, menaced both by the faintness of the erasable pencil and by the inflammable nature of the wood which is destined to be transformed into smoke. One more message in danger – as fragile as the others. Just because the signature below this message is declared by Conrad to be illegible, the word should not lead us to believe that its author was incapable of signing correctly. Illegible – eligible – chosen for this purpose, a signature which cannot be identified or imitated. Before finding the book, then, we must, as in most initiation myths, go through a doorway: 'A torn curtain of red twill hung in the doorway of the hut, and flapped sadly in our faces.' The piece of red twill is as much a symbol as the sadly tattered flag: not as melancholy perhaps, but more aggressive. It slaps the face of the intruder (the sanctuary must always be on its guard) and is still red, which is no longer true of the flag. A torn curtain – that is to say, a sign, a new possibility for the pilgrims to intrepret the ultimate sense of the quest. (It is true that text and material are in intimate harmony in this story.) Note also that the hut, like the flag and the curtain, is described as decrepit and that we are never far from whiteness: 'we could see that a white man had lived there not very long ago'. Of course Marlow, who 'spins a yarn', is not conscious of the pattern of this fine-meshed net which, unknown to him, is being woven around him. The silence of the text, the whiteness which menaces it, is more dangerous and more complex than the silence which from time to time marks the story when the voice of Marlow seems to fade away.

And here at last is the book, the 'missing clue' which is the last in a long series of coded messages, even if in the material order of things the voyage seems to be a short one. This distortion of time and space is one of the principal qualities of the story which has never really been treated adequately. The difference between the surface images which Marlow, with few interruptions, projects for his audience and their real significance which must be interpreted, constitutes the artistry and originality of the text. (There are only fifty miles from the Inner Station to the reed hut but the distance is even shorter in the reader's imagination.) The territory covered by the voyage is at the same time very limited and capable of being extended indefinitely. Marlow seizes upon the book, which, like the other symbols, seems to be tattered and torn. The cover is missing and the pages are dirty. This time, however, there is a positive element: 'but the back had been lovingly stitched afresh with white cotton thread which looked clean yet'. In this network of symbols which bear the marks of passing time and which are menaced with extinction, this is something new. We must be wary of Conrad's irony, however. Is it not strange that the most revealing clue is found not inside the book but on its back cover, a message sewn with white thread – Ariadne's clew of thread? As the invisible narrator said at the outset, it is not the content of the story which intrigues Marlow, but what lies outside it and envelops it, its nutshell. And it was at that very moment that the invisible narrator himself dropped out of the story . . . *he* is the one who is interested in the back covers of old books, not Marlow! Marlow is completely absorbed by the navigation manual written in English, but this brief moment of happiness which he experiences has ironic undertones nonetheless. Marlow believes he is on solid ground with the English of seamen and the sea. Marlow, BEWARE! This 'literature' is a piece of colonial propaganda which has been spared miraculously, far from the real world. We must not follow the example of Marlow who reads the book out of context.

This, apparently, is the only means he has of finding a moment of respite – a moment of selfish and outmoded happiness. We cannot forget that the manual is both useless and absurd and treats only of the sea when Marlow has to deal with an uncharted river. This is the first problem. Secondly, the name of the author, 'a man Tower, Towson – some such name' is another indication of the book's absurdity. Man-Tower is Towerman, a signalman in railroad terms, or a man whose head is upside-down! Thus Marlow reads backwards and misses the point entirely. In this book there is no message, no useful indication, no signal and no directions given, unless we take into account the absence of directions. Even if he is a good storyteller, Marlow is a poor reader. And if one reads out of context, one must suffer the consequences. This cotton thread, this clew of Ariadne, which serves as the binding for the damaged manual, not only leads us to the young Russian harlequin, the faithful servant of Kurtz (the notes in cipher in the margins are another indication of his presence), but is also used to spin another pattern of the text, that of slavery. The cotton worsted which the dying slave at the central station in the ravine wears as a charm around his neck is a sign of his alienation – a weightless fetter but a fetter none the less. The story is double-woven and the finished material is reversible. What exactly is the book about, anyway? What passages retain Marlow's attention? The answer is simple, a long description of chains and cables: 'This simple old sailor with his talk of chains and purchases, made me forget the jungle and the pilgrims in a delicious sensation of having come upon something unmistakably real.' Poor Marlow does not realise that the text is giving way under him. Purchase and slavery are the themes which we find on the reverse side of the text and both are underlined by the reference to chains. Marlow is off course; he is daydreaming when he reads the 'innocent' pages of the old manual and misses its significance entirely. The Guide to Navigation has washed up with its sacred tables, a survivor of the Deluge, in the centre of Africa, the new Ararat. It was not on board Noah's ark but on the colonial ships sent by the European powers, the ships which are responsible for the economic development of the capitalist nations, whose power is steam power. Do not forget the sign on the woodpile which linked writing to steam or the seaman's explanation of purchase and chains, which are ambiguous in the context of the story and which encourage the reader to reflect on political problems. No book is entirely innocent. The Bible of navigation is also a Bible of colonisation, of commerce and of the Empire. Africa is part of the Empire and one of its signs. The bible of Livingstone is translated, and betrayed, into the language of slavery and of commerce. Thus, instead of playing its proper role of reassuring symbol, instead of being a heraldic emblem representing the heraldry of the Book, the book is only absurd and meaningless – guilty, if you will. It is not a guidebook but a trap at the crossroads of the quest, not a book of healing but a log-book in which to note blunders and altered courses.

THE ROUND TABLE

Not only are the places and scenes in 'Heart of Darkness' borrowed from the romance tradition, but the characters as well. Yet, in the

case of the characters, the difference between the model and the
imitation is even more outrageous. The pilgrims, who with their
staves walk around the edge of the station, are faint and ironic
replicas of the knights who set out to find the Holy Grail: 'They
wandered here and there with their absurd long staves in their
hands, like a lot of faithless pilgrims bewitched inside a rotten fence.'
They are knights without horses to mount in a country fit only for
the donkey of a Sancho Panza, knights with unwieldy wooden
lances who are unable, as they prove innumerable times during the
story, to make efficient use of weapons, knights turning aimlessly in
circles in a Congolese Tintagel: 'they were all waiting – all the
sixteen or twenty pilgrims of them – for something'. Absurd
counterparts for Marlow and his serious undertaking, they are the
ones who will acompany him and aid him on his quest. They are
parameters of powerlessness but they take the measure of Marlow
who believes all the while that he is taking theirs. And they follow
him like his own shadow. When Marlow manages, with his Belgian
friend, to 'fish his command' from the bottom of the river, he does it
as a king of fishermen. It is with ironic intent that Marlow baptises
his fellow voyagers and makes knights of them in order to better
preserve the essence of his quest. He is careful to point out that it is
simply a rhetorical antiphrasis, that they do not have the physical
make-up of knights, that to become a knight one should not be fat,
nervous, and the proud owner of a moustache. Marlow wants it to
be understood that by contrast his own quest is a worthy and noble
one. He is wasting his breath. Even though he insists upon his own
superiority, on his capacity for useful endeavours, and on his desire
to restore life, he cannot prevent the text from taking its revenge.
The pilgrims who never leave his side and travel on the same
steamer with him are constantly judging him. Even though he keeps
his distance from them by means of his ironic attitude, they continue
to follow him. When Marlow baptises them pilgrims, they take on
the quality of symbols; reappearing as themselves at various stages
of the narration, they are carried forward by the story and take on
an allegorical function. It is true that Marlow is the victim of his
own irony – and this is the principal difficulty of the text – but his
comments must none the less be taken seriously. In a certain sense
Marlow is much like the tightrope walker of his anecdote who
cannot always give a perfect performance: 'I felt often its mysterious
stillness watching me at my monkey tricks, just as it watches you
fellows performing on your respective tight-ropes for – what is it?

half-a-crown a tumble. . . . ' Even if, in his role of innocent narrator, Marlow is not completely in control of his text – the written word is more profound and more complex than speech and often allows a wider diversity of interpretations – he controls it sufficiently to allow a naïve interpretation. On this level, there is no doubt that the pilgrims do not correspond at all to the romantic image that the Victorians had of colonial enterprises in general. That is what Marlow is saying from the depths of his irony.

The director of the Central Station is hardly the type of leader who, in the minds of most Europeans, is normally chosen to head the colonial effort after receiving an excellent preparation in European schools. We can object, of course, that these civil servants are Belgians and that Marlow is English, but that does not change the fact that the legend of the great leader, of whom Stanley is the most outstanding example, is certainly ridiculed in the portrait of the mediocre director. What qualifications are necessary, then, for a brilliant career in the colonies where a man knows he will be surrounded by savage races? Popular opinion, carefully coached by the press and a certain kind of literature, replies as with one voice: 'guts'. According to the director of the Central Station, however, that is exactly the organ which one must do without in order to survive: 'Men who come out here should have no entrails.' There is nothing exceptional in this man who is not a leader of men: 'He was commonplace in complexion, in feature, in manners, and in voice. He was of middle size and of ordinary build.' The only possible reference to epic status in his case was the round table which he had had made: 'When annoyed at meal times by the constant quarrels of the white men about precedence, he ordered an immense round table to be made for which a special house had to be built.' Now the myth of the round table has survived uninterrupted to modern times and has never lost its aura of political wisdom. There were innumerable round tables to which the European powers were convened to divide up the African continent, for example, not only are the myths dissipated and the tables turned, but savagery, all the more insidious because one is not aware of it, lurks in the background – a degradation of the Last Supper and the Communion of the Apostles. Does this communal structure for white men in the centre of Africa really justify the anthropological changes that Europe was supposed to bring to that continent? Are not the pilgrims of progress blinded by their light, the pilgrims of

Good Friday obsessed by gluttonous appetites, the pilgrims of harmony divided and in continual disagreement?

THE HOLY GRAIL

The Grail, a vase that was supposed to have contained the blood of Christ, was present in all the quests of the Arthurian knights, but only those knights protected by their innocence or their ignorance were allowed to see it. In the version of Chrétien de Troyes, Perceval, a rough and simple man, encounters the apparition at the beginning of his career:

> The Holy Grail which preceded was made of the purest gold; it was covered with precious stones, the most varied assortment of the finest gems that can be found in the earth or under the sea; no brilliance can compare to that of the Holy Grail.[8]

The Grail is a marvellous image from the East which appears at the crossroads of commerce and religion. A funeral urn covered with precious gems, it is the image of rare perfection, with both a real and a symbolic value. At times the Grail appears to the knights who, like Perceval, often realise the full significance of their experience too late; at other times, Christ himself is the object of the quest. Just as we have counterfeit pilgrims who close the procession behind Marlow and Kurtz in the heart of Africa, so we have in 'Heart of Darkness' a fraudulent imitation of the Grail. In Conrad's story, the Grail is not the gold but the ivory which all the outposts, and agents venerate and to which they are completely devoted: 'The word ivory rang in the air, in murmurs and in sighs.' The legend of the ivory replaces the legend of the Holy Grail just as the civil servants take the place of the knights; the treasure of Kurtz has the value of the Holy Sepulchre, and when we come within view of Kurtz we are invited to what can be termed a resurrection: 'His covering had fallen off, and his body emerged from it pitiful and appalling as from a winding-sheet.' Kurtz looms out of his winding-sheet much as Christ appears suddenly over the Holy Grail: 'They saw above the Grail a naked man whose feet, hands and body were bleeding.' [9] But Christ the Mystical Lamb, lives and gives his body and blood to his disciples. Kurtz is the image of death itself, a skeleton of the Last Judgement: ' I could see the cage of his ribs all astir, the bones of his

arm waving.' In the case of Kurtz the process of transubstantiation
is reversed. Kurtz, whose flesh has withered away, no longer seems
to have a human physique; worse than that, his body has solidified,
fossilised, and taken on the consistence of an object. Instead of a vase
which takes on human form, we have a human being transformed
into a statue; instead of a God become Man, a man who becomes an
idol: 'the wilderness had patted him on the head, and behold, it was
like a ball – an ivory ball; it had caressed him, and – lo! he had
withered.' Thus it is by means of his ironic use of romance traditions
that Conrad makes us understand how far the colonial quest has
deviated from its original course. It has become a vulgar material
venture and not the spiritual process of enlightenment that it was
made out to be by the Western powers. The colonial enterprise was
supposed to be one of the great adventures of Christian civilisation,
on a par with the Crusades both in imagery and in ideology, but
Conrad's treatment of it underlines the deformed image of both. By
showing us the solid block of ivory which Kurtz has become,
Conrad shows us all the brilliance of the various facets of his irony.
In Central Africa, Kurtz is a demon among demons and his lack of
interest in his material well-being resembles sainthood so closely
that it could be mistaken for it. Whiter than the missionaries of the
Holy Ghost known familiarly as the White Fathers, thinner than the
most foolish of the fools for Christ, he has, in his asceticism,
accomplished all the stages of the Imitation and become an
ultimate, incomparable model. Like the mystics who undergo the
dark night of the soul, he has, by fusion and communion, attained a
rare degree of purity and concentration. Dressed like Galahad, the
only knight to be found worthy of the Grail, his ivory armour is
impenetrable. In reality, however, this 'angel' is a beast of legend
whose mouth devours all that it encounters: 'I saw him open his
mouth wide – it gave him a weirdly voracious aspect, as though he
had wanted to swallow all the air, all the earth, all the men before
him.' His white helmet, symbol of knighthood, masks the mouth of
the bottomless pit. The confusion is such, the line between purity
and monstrosity so thinly drawn, that all the springs of classical
Christianity seem to have broken down. Kurtz marks the end of an
era, the one which opens with the Crusades in the Western world –
the era of division between day and night, between East and West.
In its most outrageous distortion, in the naïve imagery representing
him as a knight who gives combat to the Hydra, this dissociation
disappears. It is the task of Marlow/Sancho Panza for Kurtz/Don

Quixote, to scramble the codes, to close the door swinging open between Heaven and Hell, to complete the epic. Marlow, is an iconoclast in spite of himself. In that respect, he confirms the nature of his personal quest whose trajectory covers less theological ground and whose use of geography is profane. We can consider the colonial exploration of the last century as the last manifestation of all those quests whose model is found in chivalric romance.

5 Reversals

As we have seen, there are deviations, detours in 'Heart of Darkness' because traditional signs and codes have lost their original meaning and things are not what they seem to be. In deviating from the established tradition, Conrad makes new use of the trappings of romance, but does not ridicule them. He has no intention of writing farce or parody but wishes to indicate by his subtle metamorphosis that they can no longer be accepted at face value and that it is no longer possible to use the traditional passages of romance without first asking a series of pertinent questions. Elements of parody and grotesque images do appear in 'Heart of Darkness' but it is essential to separate those which are inferior to the code from those which are superior to it. On an inferior plane, Carlier and Kayerts, the Bouvards and Pécuchets of the jungle, or the leaders of the Eldorado Expedition, certainly seem to be caricatures. From the outset, their backgrounds and training condemn them to misplay the romantic roles they have chosen. On a superior plane, we have Kurtz, who lives his passion for ivory to the utmost, goes to the end of the night and falls outside the law, outside the code. He is at odds with what he says. Two different kinds of darkness are found in the story. Lack of intelligence causes some characters to misinterpret the code, while superior intelligence allows others to twist its meaning to suit their own purposes and pretend at the same time to remain faithful to it. In the eyes of the law, Kurtz is not a criminal, only a remarkable and extremely successful agent. No inquiry about him will be held. The colonial powers dreamed of finding more agents like him whose intelligence and sense of profit would work wonders for them as Kurtz had done. The language of progress is simply a subtle mask which allows them to better exploit their new territories. There are those who see through the mask just as there are those, like the Bouvards and Pécuchets, new to the written word and consequently doing their best to imitate Don Quixote, who take it as the gospel truth. As for Marlow, he falls somewhere between the two. He knows that words can have several meanings, but his existentialist morals, his commitment to his cause and his sense of responsibility (a river pilot, isn't he?) seem to be the cause of a different kind of blindness. Eventually, Marlow will discover these double meanings in spite of himself, but for the moment it is his duty to advance. Progress in his case has nothing to do, as his aunt might wish, with progress in general. If he unravels the clew of Ariadne for us, if he can be compared to the shuttle of the loom which weaves the pattern of the story, he is at no time responsible for the choice of the pattern. That is why 'blindness' should not be considered as more important than it really is. Marlow is simply the naïve observer who enables the story to move forward. Apparently neutral, he accepts without blinking the co-existence of the language of progress and the exploitation of the African continent. When he makes articulate comparisons with the romantic tradition, however, his degree of consciousness is more difficult to evaluate. It would seem that he compares his own voyage to a classic quest of deliverance: 'The approach to this Kurtz grubbing for ivory in the wretched bush was beset by as many dangers as though he had been an enchanted princess sleeping in a fabulous castle.' Marlow is hardly a princess and even less of a sleeping beauty unless we take into account amateurs of obscure texts on the look-out for perverted quest. In this statement, Marlow seems to analyse the nature of his journey and in the same breath to undermine its aura of mystery. Marlow knows his *Ivanhoe* and deliberately changes it. As to whether the choice of words is calculated as well, that is another story entirely. There are two kinds of whiteness in the text which do not go well together—that of the ivory, the colour of the tower, the colour of dream in which princesses are captive (note the use of the archaic term 'beset') and that of earth-coloured larva or grub. There is a conflict between an airy and celestial whiteness and a mortal wormlike one. There is a short-circuiting of the two impulses in the story, the noble quest undertaken out of love and the vile adventure undertaken for base material reasons. This particular larva will develop into a terrifying monster. All these detours have the effect of making the text obscure, whereas in the romance tradition a sovereign language made everything clear. The detours confuse those who follow the quest, whereas the Glorious Way penetrated to the very heart of the forest. There is, however, another consequence which is even more radical and even more paradoxical, one that coincides with the flattening out of the two different levels on which the story is told to one single plane. Conrad is not satisfied with deviating from the code, with putting together the superior and the inferior, the pure and the impure; he goes one step further. Like a dealer in a card game he turns over the flattened surface; and, in so doing, he turns the images upside-down and knocks from their pedestals some of the most revered idols of the Empire.

'CIVIS ROMANUS SUM'

That was the reply of Saint Paul to those who came to arrest him. He was telling them that a citizen of Rome enjoyed immunity from arrest. In the nineteenth century, British citizens enjoyed a similar status in foreign countries:

> A British citizen living in a foreign country was able to pride himself on being a citizen of a world power whose reputation and worldwide influence was sufficient protection under any and all circumstances. He too, would be able to reply, as Saint Paul had: 'Civis Romanus sum'.[1]

During his quest, a similar sense of personal immunity greatly influences Marlow's conduct. Like the most famous heroes of adventure literature, he throws himself headlong into dangerous situations and manages to come out alive. Surrounded by falsehood and false heroism which have been 'made in Europe', he keeps his distance and integrity. Everywhere he goes he is, like an impregnable island, superbly alone. This is particularly evident at the beginning of the voyage when he confesses to feelings of being an outsider on board the French ship. That is because Marlow, as a British citizen, does not feel he has anything in common with the grotesque farce which is played for his benefit against the backdrop of the forest, 'some sordid farce acted in front of a sinister backcloth', or with French and Belgian military personnel, administrators and agents. The only person with whom he feels somewhat at ease is the Swedish captain who, in his small steamer, takes him into the interior. He is a Swede; that is to say, a man who comes close to being an Englishman as far as religion and democratic customs are concerned. And yet, as the example of Fresleven aptly proves, this resemblance does not confer the same kind of immunity that Marlow has, for Fresleven, a Danish river pilot whom Marlow is going to replace, dies during a quarrel with natives about the ownership of some black hens. Scandinavians do speak English, however, even if it is their own special brand of it. The presence of the Swedish captain seems to comfort Marlow who, like Robinson Crusoe on his island, is ready to take into his heart whatever reminds him of England.

We should not really count on Marlow's being neutral or let ourselves be too easily taken in by his humanistic pronouncements. Marlow usually passes for a civilised and charitable human being in this colonial hell, but what a naïve interpretation that is. It does not take into account the 'heart of darkness'. Now, the way to Hell is paved with exactly the kind of good intentions with which Marlow is equipped. What, for example, but a good intention, gives him the idea of offering a ship's biscuit to the skeletal figure of the dying black slave? 'I found nothing else to offer to do but to offer him one of my good Swede's ship's biscuits.' No, it will not do to make of Marlow a kind of neutral inquirer, a blue helmeted member of a United Nations peacekeeping force ahead of his time. We should not speak of watchful neutrality in his case, but rather of an absence of commitment to a specific cause. Marlow arrives in Africa sure of his rights, of his personal immunity and of his superiority. Morally, he believes he is part of a just society that is incapable of wrongdoing: 'Civis Romanus sum'. And it is precisely these feelings of certitude that will disappear in Africa. They will be replaced by feelings of self-doubt and a certain appreciation of the ambiguous nature of human existence. 'Heart of Darkness' is certainly an open denunciation of the colonial adventure in Africa, but it is also a subtle attempt to get at the root of self-complacency found in Victorian society. In this sense, the beginning of the book is its ending as well. Contrary to the traditional progression of most adventure stories, both beginning and end include the presentation of a serious problem: Marlow demonstrates and remonstrates against the evils of colonisation.

Rather than going directly to the heart of the argument, which could almost be presented in the manner of a syllogism, and in order to respect the order of the text from which the argument is taken, we will use Marlow's method and concentrate, like him, on the events which make up the background of the story rather than on its actual content, on the 'shell rather than the nut'. As we well know, the narrative has multiple locations. Marlow has chosen the lower reaches of the Thames as if he intended to bring his listeners as close to the stage as possible in order to put them at the centre of the action. The Thames, of course, is a stand-in for the Congo river which Marlow the actor will travel up on his quest. Marlow has managed to assemble a quartet of well-known figures from the City on a stage set on the water, which is a particularly unstable element, and that is a performance in itself. We could even say that the banker among them has agreed to change the nature of his liquid assets . . . The banker, the lawyer, and the company director from the heart of the City, which is itself the heart of London or of England or even of the British Empire, form the chorus in the drama. They represent the City's venerable institutions which Marlow, with the humour and the clever persuasion of a detective (there is an inquisitive side to Marlow which will be more apparent in *Lord Jim*), questions indirectly. At one time or another, all of these men followed the sea: 'Between us there was as I have already said somewhere, the bond of the sea.' But not one of them, Marlow excepted, can be considered a professional: 'He was the only one of us who still followed the sea.' Having brought his listeners to his own home ground, Marlow is the undisputed master of the situation and his listeners resign themselves to listening to one of his stories: 'we knew we were fated, before the ebb began to run, to hear about one of Marlow's inconclusive experiences.' This *tour de force* which brings businessmen and bankers together for a story about the sea is of capital importance. It represents more than a change of location for them to be at sea, on the sea to which they are attached and to which they have ties but which is not their natural element. Even if we never leave the Greenwich meridian, London is not really in London. Its centre has moved. Besides, geography and space are not the only elements which undergo changes. The moment chosen is just as symbolic. Marlow waits for the incoming and the outgoing tides, the period that usually lasts about thirty minutes when the flood is over and the ebb is not yet begun: 'The flood had made, the wind was nearly calm, and being bound down the river, the only thing for it was to come and wait for the turn of the tide.' The instability of the setting on the tidal reaches corresponds to the instability of the fleeting moment. Time is running out. Already there is a new tide in the making on the horizon, already in the east the colours are beginning to change:

In the offing the sea and the sky were welded together without a joint, and in the luminous space the tanned sails of the barges drifting up with the tide seemed to stand still in red clusters of canvas sharply peaked, with gleams of varnished spirits.

Saint Elmo's fire, the genies of the fable which haunt the palace of the Princess Scheherazade in *The Thousand and One Nights*. Sea and sky, palace of purity, united completely and irrevocably but threatened with extinction and loss of consciousness (vanished/varnished): 'We live in the flicker.' Time is running out. Although his listeners are looking out to sea, towards the exotic land of their adolescence, towards the colours of 'youth', Marlow, the old follower of the sea, is going to oblige them to look inside themselves, not to make them descend into that unfamiliar hell where 'the heavens are of no consequence', but to force them to look closely into what is familiar. There is still too large a measure of exoticism in the desire of Baudelaire.

Thirty minutes, that is about the time it takes Marlow to tell his story, or almost – he does go a bit over time: 'We have lost the first of the ebb,' said the Director. This cosmic parenthesis between the tides is sufficient, however. It will give Marlow just enough time to talk about human history – the two periods of human history – outgoing and incoming. In fact, if Marlow chooses this period of calm and suspense to spin his yarn, it is certainly because we are most receptive to what is new and strange during moments of respite. But there is something else as well. In the period between the tides time is not only suspended, but, like the very waters of the tides, unites two opposing factors as well. For a brief moment, time has been stopped and the contradictions between those opposites have been resolved in a non-dialectic manner. It is a period of equilibrium between opposite poles of attraction. And the story which Marlow tells during the thirty minutes of calm is a story which goes out and comes in again. The two periods no longer use the established rhythms, however, but appear almost simultaneously. The story of an outgoing current is conditioned by the story of an incoming one. It is the history of the colonial process which, after a period of prosperity, begins to decline. Marlow's voyage up-river shows the full extent of that disintegration. Before uniting these two forms of time in the dramatic movement of the narration, however, Conrad is careful, like the dedicated teacher that he is, to present them separately. This period of equilibrium between the tides, then, is not only the stage or a simple backdrop for the action, but has a role to play in the story itself. It is a metaphor for the ideas which are developed in the tale. That is why Conrad opens his story with an anonymous reverie about the Thames – anonymous, that is, unless we take into account the invisible narrator sitting in the shadows next to his colleagues from the City. Is the invisible narrator supposed to be Conrad? It is far more likely that Conrad is multiplying the number of masks. After all, Africa is the continent of masks, isn't it? The naïve reverie of the invisible narrator, very much like the picture histories sold by the wandering merchants of Epinal in the nineteenth century or like the historic pageants of which the English are so fond, retraces the building of the Empire. On the royal avenue of the Thames, a kind of liquid Pall Mall, pass the silhouettes of famous navigators like Sir Francis Drake and Sir John Franklin. These knights of the sea are followed by their ships, the *Golden Hind* and the *Erebus*. The flow of the river becomes the flow of history, official history, which reflects docile time as it is inscribed, recto verso, in the history books. In this eternal golden age, in this never-ending summer where all is light, history is written as an uninterrupted series of departures, as an exhausting relay race against the night in order to maintain in all its splendour the dawn of a golden age. The conquistadors of Elizabeth I did everything in their power and sometimes managed the impossible to fill their sovereign ship, the *Golden Hind*, with gold, so that it might return ready to be visited by the Queen's Highness. (Water, light, and the music of Handel. Enter Marlow.)

It is into the midst of this glorious vision that Marlow steps with his quiet observation: ' "And this also," said Marlow suddenly, "has been one of the dark places of the earth".' Were you ready for this reversal of situation? It was quite predictable. Already a few shadows had fallen across the official representation of events. The truth will have its out even when history has been thoroughly censured. We know, for example, that Elizabeth I was not satisfied with 'welcoming' the returning ships of the Crown which were building England's first colonial empire, and, when she felt it necessary, did not hesitate to 'welcome' a captain like Sir Walter Raleigh with a reprimand (to visit/visitation). Furthermore, where we would expect to find the traditional phrase 'messengers of light' for these explorers, a slight slip of the tongue changes them into 'messengers of might'. When the text slips again, it is even more revealing because it occurs at the close of a rhetorical passage. That famous image of colonial dissemination, the 'seeds of empires' become the victim of a curious infection which transforms them into 'germs of empires', so that the text bears not only the mark of its ambiguity but of its vanity. What a contrast with the glorious scenes from official history, full of pomp and circumstance, with their long lines of characters, and the low-lying sandbanks and marshes of the Thames reaches where the glorious spirit of the past is evoked. We find once again the contamination of what is superior with what is inferior, of what is noble by what is not. The ambiguity and the vanity of official history are united in a striking image. When the heroic reverie of the invisible narrator comes to an end, there is silence once again, and then the scenery itself comes to the foreground. The sun has set, dusk is falling and already ships' lights, the promise of stories to come, appear on the 'fairway' of the river. The brightest light of all comes from a lighthouse: 'The Chapman lighthouse, a three-legged thing erect on a mud-flat, shone strongly.' It is an ambiguous light with a symbolic name indicating someone halfway between adolescence and maturity and, like all the signals of history, it is a vain light as well. Standing on a century of mud, it is a mortal lighthouse with feet of clay.

Thus the invisible narrator had involuntarily prepared the scene for Marlow. Marlow brings with him the incoming tide; he brings the night. Instead of fulfilling the expectations raised by the ships' lights dispersed on the river like so many genies from *The Thousand and One Nights*, Marlow's story, a disappointing one, will put out the lights one by one. Marlow is as dull as ditchwater. The reversal of the situation, for which he alone is responsible, has two phases. First of all, the official version of the history of the first colonial conquests, which the invisible narrator set in the reign of Elizabeth I, was merely an attempt to gild the lily. Instead of adding to the lustre of the Elizabethan era, a different setting is introduced quietly and without attracting attention.

The change of scene takes only a few moments but the story changes direction entirely, changes its course, if you will. The displacement of a company director, a lawyer, and a banker has the effect of symbolically removing the City from its unmovable base, from its position at the centre of the universe, and of announcing the direction which Marlow's story will take. Instead of choosing as a backdrop the golden screen of the Elizabethan era, he sets the City, London and England in an age when they were only outposts of Rome, to which all roads led. In Marlow's version, England becomes once again an uncharted territory subject to the yoke of colonisation, where there is no light, only darkness: 'Light came out of this river since – you say Knights?' Knights/nights, another slight slip of the tongue from Conrad/Marlow – there is a world of difference between the two, isn't there?

At this point in his story, Marlow pauses in order not to upset his listeners and to introduce another romantic image, that of a Roman soldier stationed in the barbarian land of England. The Roman soldier, a favourite choice of Victorian authors.[2] In one of Kipling's stories, the centurion is so deeply attached to the conquered territory and to the colonial soil, that he decides not to return to Rome with his legion when the term of his service is at an end. It is very cleverly done. Kipling's Roman soldier has nothing but love and veneration in his heart for England; it is thinly disguised pious English patriotism in Roman costume; an Englishman disguised as a Roman makes his declaration to another England, India. If Kipling cleverly combines love of country and colonies in his work, the ordinary Roman soldier holds no interest for Conrad. The members of the Roman military whom he imagines are the commander of a trireme and a young citizen who, because of his gambling debts, had no other choice but to enlist in the Legion. Conrad is not interested in the devotion to the Empire which Kipling propagates. He is preoccupied by the fact that the future builders of the Roman Empire are so poorly equipped for their task. The men with the military training will perhaps be more successful than the civilians because of their ability to follow orders, their sense of discipline or, to put it more bluntly, their lack of imagination. Marlow does not say so in so many words but he does suggest it. The civilians are more vulnerable than the soldiers because of the very reasons which have sent them to the colonies, the necessity of mending their fortunes or their ways. In returning to the past, to the England of the Romans, Marlow introduces the second phase of his reversal of the situation.

The Victorian listeners are not surprised at all by this reference to Rome and Roman Wars. Was not the British Empire in the nineteenth century the greatest empire the world had known since Rome? Did not Victorian philosophers like Carlyle hold up the Roman virtues as models? Therefore, in order to prevent his listeners from identifying themselves completely with the Roman conquerors, Marlow is obliged to take certain preventive measures. He has to convert his listeners from the cult of Rome and things Roman. He must not allow them to pay a disguised tribute to a conquest by force. He is trying to make them feel vulnerable and even frighten them if he can:

> Well, if a lot of mysterious niggers armed with all kinds of fearful
> weapons suddenly took to travelling on the road between Deal
> and Gravesend, catching the yokels right and left to carry heavy
> loads for them, I fancy every farm and cottage thereabouts would
> get empty very soon. ('Heart of Darkness', p. 70).

Using the military metaphor suggested by the text, we could say
that Conrad employs a definite strategy of writing in this passage,
one which consists mainly in using clichés ironically. We need to
take a closer look at Conrad's strategy when he invites the reader to
look at the other side of the question. What, he suggests, if the
invader were not Roman at all but Black, the representative of
slavery and darkness: 'Well, if a lot of mysterious niggers . . . '
Here, the audience, whose latent racism cannot tolerate such a
possibility, revolts.

In spite of a few grumblings, Marlow's listeners are usually quite
patient and do hear him out to the end of his tale. They are listening
but the author is modest enough to realise that his arguments may
not be of much consequence.

What Marlow actually proposes to his listeners is Kipling's world
turned upside-down and inside-out, a world where all the roads no
longer lead to Rome. The paradox of Marlow is voluntarily
ambiguous. These 'niggers', whose invasion he imagines ironically,
are only disguised Romans. (Let us render unto Caesar what is
Caesar's . . .) If we accept the historical relationship established
by the Victorians, these 'niggers' can only be Romans in disguise.
Consequently, Conrad is using prejudice to combat prejudice. First
of all, where does he have the invaders land? At Deal: that is to say,
where it is supposed that the troops of Caesar landed during their
first reconnaissance of English territory. And what social class does
Conrad have them meet? Elizabethan yokels who are ready for the
yoke, the Roman yoke. Conrad plays with history, upsetting myths
and debunking official propaganda, letting his troublemakers loose
in Deal just as Henri Michaux lets camels loose in Honfleur. We are
dealing with serious political satire. Several points will make this
perfectly clear. First of all, the Roman colonists treat the natives
cruelly, just as the English treated the Africans in Victoria's time.
Secondly, the English natives are portrayed as victims who haven't
the means to resist the Roman invader. Only colonial propaganda

can possibly, for the needs of the cause, consider the Elizabethan yokels as enemies. It is ridiculous to describe their pitiful means of defence as 'fearful weapons' and to compare their arms to the destructive power of the arms furnished by a powerful industrial nation. And last of all, the Roman colonists have no heart and no love for their fellow man; their strength and power are 'just an accident arising from the weakness of others'. In this way, Conrad turns the weapon of racial prejudice against those who wield it. He puts his adversaries on the defensive and shows them the baseness of their point of view. Here lies the real tragedy: the powerful can only imagine that they are weak in a negative sense, defensively. For Conrad, nationalism is a land of myth and make-believe. Because the Roman Empire is based on force, he does not accept the false universality of 'Civis Romanus sum'. Travelling in the centre of Africa with his halo of immunity, like a hero, like a saint, Marlow is really the representative of a powerful colonial power even if he minimises that aspect of his English heritage and does not fully admit to himself the extent of his own association with it. He is the representative of colourless nationalism diluted in the universality of the colonial process.

'MR STANLEY, I PRESUME?'

In a chapter of his recent work on Livingstone, Tim Jeal reminds us of the immediate success of this famous aphorism pronounced by Stanley at Ujiji when he first met Livingstone.[3] He is giving the Victorians credit for an extremely well-developed sense of humour, however, when he affirms that this short statement was received in England with a unanimous burst of laughter.

We can ask ourselves if Tim Jeal does not project on the Victorians the incredulity which we ourselves experience when we encounter the posturing and hollow words of the time. It is possible that, as was frequently the case in England, the success of the phrase with journalists and magazine writers may have been a form of sentimental sympathy which they could not express in any other way. In this regard, 'Heart of Darkness' undertakes a complete, 'heartbreaking' investigation of Stanley's cliché that is far more convincing than a simple quotation spoken 'tongue in cheek' – a facial expression which, after all, is only the other side of a stiff upper lip. (It is exactly the opposite – a reversal.) What interests Conrad is not so much the words themselves as the context in which they were spoken. We can assume beyond the shadow of a doubt that 'Heart of Darkness' is a systematic contradiction of the remark, which had already acquired the status of a 'cliché'. For Conrad, the words masked Stanley's real efforts. Tim Jeal shows us how Stanley repeated his lines like an actor with a bad case of stage-fright. Television cameras were not on the scene to film the event, of course, but Stanley, like any hero of the day with a good stage sense, was conscious of making history:

> Fearing to lose his prestige as a white man in this extraordinary circumstance if he allowed any trace of emotion to appear on his features, he tried to imagine what a member of the aristocracy would have said and done in a similar situation.

We should also read the entire chapter concerning the preparations for the expedition in order to understand the role of the press in this affair and especially that of the director of the *New York Herald*, a certain Mr Bennet, who calculated Stanley's chances of rescue with a mixture of cynicism and cleverness. Conrad's approach to myth-making is quite justified in 'Heart of Darkness'. Africa is a theatre where a farce is being played and we cannot find fault with prose which tries to do away with the empty rhetoric which accompanied the colonical advance. Stanley, like Julien Sorel, practised his speeches in front of the mirror . . . history is written just like a novel. In order to arrive on the scene for the culminating point of his career, Henry Morton Stanley followed the itinerary of the hero of a novel. A quest for a name, for an identity, the route of Stanley is that of an illegitimate child, according to Marthe Robert.[4] Like a hero of antiquity, he was abandoned first by his mother and then by his family and finally given shelter by a sinister disciplinary home, one of those famous workhouses where the heroes of Dickens went at least once as boarders during their childhood. Stanley tried to kill his adoptive father, the director of the institution, left him for dead, and found a ship in Liverpool which took him to America. Serving first on one side then on the other, on land and then at sea, during the American Civil War, he later switched to journalism and tried to forget the past. His reconciliation with his mother country had to take place in Africa. Like a modern Telemachus, he left Zanzibar at the head of a colossal expedition and went into the heart of Africa looking for his father.

If Stanley played the role of the son with zeal, Livingstone was just as good as the father. A ghostly being lost in the underbrush of the jungle, he was waiting for some Hamlet to come and deliver him. Like the God of Genesis taking the air at dusk in the Garden of Eden, he called to his children who had sinned in a voice full of misericorde, hoping to free them from the effects of the Fall so that they would turn their faces towards him. He was the founding father, the figurehead which the colonial effort needed in order to continue unhindered. After all, what could be more venerable than this explorer who had gone to the last frontiers of the unknown, more inspiring than this apostle who had been exposed to martyrdom daily among the savages? As Tim Jeal explains, it was not important that this expedition was a scientific failure. What was important was that Livingstone had gone to the source of the Nile, to the source of nothingness. Livingstone had gone to death's door with a barely audible dream of water: 'Is this the Luapula?' and had struck the Victorian imagination indelibly. His adventure was transformed into a myth with multiple meanings and applications. The most famous of them was perhaps Kipling's *Kim*, in which an old Tibetan lama followed inexorably his dream of finding a sacred river. There is another side to the myth of Livingstone, however. As Tim Jeal shows, the other side was not the most important side, but there were some chinks in the armour of the Victorian knight who never returned from the other side of the mirror. In real life, Livingstone was not a good father. History really is stranger than fiction. Isn't it astonishing that Robert Livingstone, the son of the explorer, whom his father had left, as we might say, to himself was, like Stanley, enrolled in the federal army during the American Civil War? The prediction of Livingstone, 'I am at my wit's end, my impossible son has enlisted in the American army and is going to be used as fertilizer for the battlefields', turned out to be quite accurate and Livingstone's remorse was all the greater when he learned that his son had actually been kidnapped in Natal, now South Africa, and forced to enlist in the northern armies. It is not improbable that Stanley, a survivor of the Civil War, seemed to Livingstone to be a long-lost son or even a prodigal one. Truth and fiction are inextricably intertwined in the relationship of Stanley and Livingstone, to such a degree that it is no longer possible to separate them or to distinguish myth from reality.

In 'Heart of Darkness' however, Conrad tries to do precisely that by turning 'old clichés' inside-out and upside-down. First of all, he

reverses the order of the quest. Instead of having Stanley go to meet
Livingstone, Livingstone goes to meet Stanley. Still wearing the
halo of immunity conferred on him by his British citizenship,
Marlow, who resembles Livingstone, goes to the heart of the jungle
to meet Kurtz. Marlow's encounter at the Inner Station with the
dying slaves brings to mind the descriptions left by Livingstone
about the bad treatment meted out to Black slaves by their Arab
masters: 'With frightening regularity, they discovered other bodies,
some had been killed with knifeblows, others by bullets, many of
them had been tied together and allowed to die of hunger.'

Just Like Livingstone, Marlow is helpless when confronted with
such a disaster. His Christian charity, like the biscuit which he gives
to the dying slave, can only be symbolic. When he sets out to find
Kurtz, Marlow believes that he is advancing toward a legendary
figure, but he meets up with a brute, with a Stanley. The brutality of
Stanley is, in fact, well established but most accounts do not insist
upon it. Tim Jeal mentions his love of the whip. In this book *The
White Nile*,[5] Alan Moorhead describes the episode in Bumbire
where Stanley, in order to take his revenge for a less than cordial
welcome, turned the cannon against warriors armed only with
lances. These anecdotes are told with discretion. The chroniclers of
Stanley do not insist upon them but upon his astonishing efficiency,
and take care to attribute his brutality to his long years of hardship.
This attempt to whitewash Stanley does not succeed and just goes to
prove how close the ties really were between the colonial system and
the repressive society of the period.

In 'Heart of Darkness', Livingstone advances toward Stanley,
but Conrad does not limit his paradox to a simple dramatic reversal.
In his eyes, there is much more than a myth to overturn. Conrad
intends to prove that a kind of complicity, reproducing the real
complicity which existed between Livingstone and Stanley, unites
Marlow and Kurtz. If we limited our analysis to the dramatic
intrigue only, we would be tempted to conclude that when Marlow/
Livingstone came back to Africa to see with his own eyes the results
of the enterprise he had begun, he discovered with horror that the
humanitarian principles which had guided the spirit of his adventure had been trampled to the ground by his successors, by all these
Kurtz/Stanleys. We could even compare Marlow to an explorer like
Brazza who, at the close of his career, when asked by the French
government to investigate the Congo affair, was so disappointed by
the results of the colonisation which had begun in peace, that he

went back to Dakar to die.[6] For Conrad, 'Heart of Darkness' is intended to be much more than the story of disappointment and bitterness (we must attribute to the author the last words pronounced by Kurtz: 'The horror, The horror!'), more than a question of a simple deviation from principles which were poorly understood or poorly applied, more than a simple error in the course of events that it would still be possible to make up for. It is the very principle of colonisation itself, as well as its origins, which Conrad condemns. When Marlow, like Saint Christopher, takes Kurtz on his shoulders and brings him back to the steamer bending under the weight of his burden, we are certainly aware of the reference to Christian hagiography, but we should not be content with seeing in it a simple act of charity in the purest tradition of saintliness, for it is never a question of reading 'Heart of Darkness' as an illustration of the Redemption. The myths used in the story are the basic myths of Western culture taken from the Greek and Latin literature which has been left to us by Dante, Shakespeare, the Romantic poets, and even Flaubert, who all used them in a personal way.

Conrad refines the myths to their barest outlines, multiplies their number, contrasts them, and goes to the limits of what Western culture can express. In this instance, the image of Marlow carrying the 'child' Kurtz on his shoulders serves to underline the blind complicity which leads Marlow towards Kurtz, the paralysed one, Livingstone towards Stanley. It is the image of an image which acts as a lever to debunk the complacent 'clichés' which had been thrown at the feet of the archetype. Expressions such as 'the White man's burden' are distorted as well in 'Heart to Darkness': the White man has no other burden than that of another White man. Scattered to the winds as well are the images of progress in which Whites, the petty albino kings of the forest, travel in their carrying chairs. Vanished also the image of Livingstone dying on a stretcher carried on Black shoulders, then dead, in his winding sheet and taken, like a sacred mummy, to Zanzibar by his faithful servants. Colonisation has become an affair for White people only, from which the Black races are excluded.

Kurtz and Marlow, these two halves of the West, are complementary and inseparable. Turn over Marlow and you have Kurtz. The other side of Livingstone is Stanley. Angel and beast cannot be separated. If Marlow decides to hide the truth from the fiancée of Kurtz, it is not out of Christian charity, but out of obedience to a bigger lie, the Occidental lie which Marlow does not feel strong enough to refute and with which he feels he has ties. It would seem that Conrad wished to show that the colonialism of Stanley was written in the inaugural gesture of Livingstone, that the son continued the work of the father and that the voyage of Marlow returning to Kurtz could be understood as the itinerary of a Livingstone returning to find his origins, trying to understand them through the actions of the son Kurtz/Stanley. Wasn't it the ultimate reward for a man who was obsessed until his last dying breath by finding the source of the Nile? Conrad reveals in this story that he is a dedicated iconoclast – in the literal sense of the word. Dissipating myths and the rhetoric of colonial progress which flourished in an Empire where its real significance was hidden, questioning ideals which are really no more than abstract forms of idols, as Marlow remarks at the beginning of the quest:

> The conquest of the earth, which mostly means the taking it away from those who have a different complexion or slightly flatter noses than ourselves, is not a pretty thing when you look into it too much. What redeems it is the idea only. An idea at the back of it; not a sentimental pretence but an idea; an unselfish belief in the idea – something you can set up, and bow down before, and offer a sacrifice to. (p. 50)

Marlow feels that colonial ideals have a certain amount of logic which gives them coherence, but the words within the words are just so many traps which make the attempts to save the ideals quite vain. (Marlow is always ready to save someone or something.) Thus to kneel down before an idea, to 'bow down' or to offer a sacrifice to it, is not much better than idolatry. In other words, the civilised races, who use ideals as a pretext for their own type of paganism, who use the idolatry of the pagans to better subject them to the yoke and to better impose their own way of thinking, set up another kind of idol which is all the more insidious because it is coherent and refined.

The iconoclasm of Conrad appears in another sector as well, that of the scenery or backdrop. We have seen with what care Marlow/ Conrad set the scene for the narration, taking into account the place and the hour of the changing tide. His care for the details has a relationship not only to the dramatic necessity of the intrigue, but to the ideas behind it as well. In this text, it is the very theatricality of the West which is constantly in question. The power of Kurtz over his fellows and subordinates is due to his use of rhetoric, which masks his real intentions. Appearing in the lenses of Marlow's binoculars, he is like a white stone at the centre of innumerable concentric circles:

> I could not hear a sound, but through my glasses I saw the thin arm extended commandingly, the lower jaw moving, the eyes of the apparition shining darkly far in its bony head that nodded with grotesque jerks. I saw him open his mouth wide . . . A deep voice reached me faintly. He must have been shouting. (p. 133)

Living in an age of television, we could say that it is an image from which the sound has been cut. At the time when 'Heart of Darkness' was written, silent movies appeared for the first time. Whatever might be their influence on this passage, the techniques which Conrad uses are displacement and distance. Kurtz, an actor among other actors, sets the stage for his own entrance, speaks a language of his own and creates a legend which, with time, is revealed to be a lie. The binoculars of Marlow still bear the imprint of the shrunken heads that he has just noticed for the first time on the stakes of the fence around the hut of this cannibal-like Robinson Crusoe (these grimacing masks of grotesque comedy resemble the skull of the buffoon which Hamlet holds). Like Stanley looking for exactly the right phrase before his meeting with Livingstone and realising that he is being watched, Kurtz creates a drama where he plays all the principal roles. A White man idolized by himself, blinded by himself, whose idealism is his most dangerous attribute, Kurtz is like Narcissus, reassured by his mirror with its silver reflections of dark-skinned faces and dark eyes. Hamlet goes up to the crenellated towers of his palace, very much like Gordon looking out over the desert before going down in his dress whites to die on the steps of a stairway – in dress whites, a suitable costume for historians and posterity: 'Did I come down the stairway with bravura?'

THE MINSTREL OF THE EAST

> A wandering minstrel I,
> A thing of shreds and patches,
> Of ballads, songs and snatches
> And dreamy lullaby.
>
> *The Mikado*[7]

If the story 'Heart of Darkness' seems to follow, on the surface at least, the logical progression of a traditional exploration, one of its elements is certainly out of harmony with the others and sounds a false note, as if it were calculated to make the story fail. It is the appearance on the scene of the young Russian explorer: 'His very existence was improbable, inexplicable and altogether bewildering,' says Marlow of him, but we must beware of Marlow. We know by now that he reads without understanding and that he is overcome on all sides by the text. Away from the narrow bridge of his steamer to which he confines himself willingly as if to a neutral territory, all languages are dead languages for him, no more than ciphers, meaningless ciphers. The story of the young Russian adventurer is one of the outgrowths of the story which Conrad is so fond of developing unknown to the characters in the story. At the very moment when the story would seem to have reached its goal at last, at the very moment when Marlow's steamer arrives within view of Kurtz, this young Russian appears suddenly out of the bush and screens us from Kurtz. More important is the fact that he takes the story off on another tack while he holds the centre of the stage and causes a delay. This minor character is conceived in the image of the notes which he scribbled in the margins of the *Inquiry Into Some Points of Seamanship*, which was discovered by Marlow at the beginning of the voyage up-river. With respect to the intrigue and to the major characters, his importance is marginal, but with his 'ciphers', he manages to introduce confusion in a Guide to Navigation which is otherwise quite clear and straightforward. By introducing this character, Conrad obliges us to make another detour. What can a Russian explorer be doing in the heart of Africa? The question would not be asked today, but in the Victorian era it was a surprising phenomenon.

In fact the young Russian has his place in the margins of the most important part of the story, just as Tsarist Russia had its place at the end of the nineteenth century as a marginal power among the major colonial powers. We are aware of the hostility declared many times by Conrad towards Russia in essays like 'Autocracy and War' for instance, and the portrait that Marlow draws for us of the explorer is of a person who is assuredly without scruples of any kind. He is very young, a man with his future ahead of him whose only motive is the need for space and virgin lands capable of quenching his thirst for adventure: 'He surely wanted nothing from the wilderness but space to breathe in and to push on through. His need was to exist, and to move onwards at the greatest possible risk, and with a maximum of privations.' In the eyes of Marlow, the representative of a nation whose most glorious hours of colonisation were already in the past and whose dawn of conquest had begun in the reign of Elisabeth I, this young Russian symbolises the reserves of energy still intact and the thirst for adventure of the Russians. Marlow, as a tired colonist of the old order, has perceived that the tide has turned, that the ebb is near, and envies the carefree attitude and the ambition unhampered by moral considerations which drives the young ambassador from the East. We could almost say that in his admiration for brute strength there is a trace of fascism in Marlow's character. We cannot, however, detect the least trace of admiration for the Russia of the Tsarist regime. There is certainly more to this passage than meets the eye. That the young explorer is Russian is only one element of his character. A marginal element if you will. The patched coat that he sports so jauntily practically contradicts his national origins. Marlow compares him to a harlequin:

> He looked like a harlequin. His clothes had been made of some stuff that was brown holland probably, but it was covered with patches all over, with bright patches, blue, red, and yellow — patches on the back, patches on the front, patches on the elbows and knees; coloured bindings around his jacket, scarlet edging at the bottom of his trousers. (p. 122)

Colours are rare in a story which uses two neutral tones of black and white, so they are all the more remarkable here. This multicoloured clothing brings to mind the map of the African colonies spotted by Marlow in the office of the Belgian company in Brussels:

> on one end a large shining map, marked with all the colours of a rainbow. There was a vast amount of red – good to see at any time, because one knows that some real work is done in there, a deuce of a lot of blue, a little green, smears of orange, and, on the East coast, a purple patch, to show where the jolly pioneer of progress drink the jolly lager-beer. However, I wasn't going into any of these. I was going into the yellow. Dead in the centre. (p. 55)

There is a difference, however, between the map and the harlequin costume. The colours of the map were given in the order of prominence of the colonial powers: red for England, blue for France, green for Portugal and orange for Holland, but they are found inextricably mixed on the large-sleeved coat. That the material is made of Dutch broadcloth goes well with the conquest of Africa, where the Boers had cut out their first colony. Thus the young Russian harlequin wears on his back the multicoloured shell of the colonial powers, the shell of an Africa which had been cut up and patched – balkanized – an Africa that had been unsewn on the green baize of a round table in Berlin in 1885. That the young explorer is Russian changes nothing. He is Russian just as the most ardent colonial ambition in 1900 and the biggest appetite for conquest are Russian. New to colonisation but trained in the most efficient methods, those of the Dutch and the English. The Dutch school is represented here by one of the older merchants whose counterparts we find in Conrad's Malay novels, a certain Van Shuyten: ' It appears he had persuaded a Dutch trading-house on the coast to fit him out with stores and tools.' The English school, whose tobacco is especially well liked by the young Russian, is also represented. It is the good tobacco of Sir Walter Raleigh, with its perfume of Virginia and slavery: 'What? Tobacco! Now, that's brotherly. Smoke? Where's a sailor that does not smoke?' This acceptance of the offer of tobacco seals the alliance between the two forms of colonialism, the older one represented by Marlow, so old that it is practically justified in its own eyes, so old that it has become colourless, odourless, and no longer has the naiveté to proclaim its presence with the loud, flamboyant colours of its flag.

The old and the new, the West and the East, this apparently, is one significance of the meeting between Marlow and the young Russian, a meeting which the reader might still see as a simple delay, gratuitous detour in the march toward Kurtz; but we must not forget that the young Russian explorer is turned towards Kurtz as well as Marlow. The young Russian is an ambiguous figure whom Marlow, representing in that respect the reactions of a reader who accepts a psychological explanation with difficulty, tries to make confess. Moreover, he is an evanescent figure whom Marlow tries to pin down, to whom he tries to give a definite form, for whom he tries to discover a human passion, a body which vanishes and hides behind the disguise of multicoloured clothing. This mötley harlequin is also a screen for Kurtz. Not only a screen destined to prevent Marlow from advancing further, not only a decoy or a lure prepared by Kurtz to fascinate Marlow or to entice him away from his guest, although that is one of the uses that the Belgian agent makes of his disciple just as he uses the tribe of warriors to persuade Marlow not to continue up-river, but rather a movie screen on which a coloured shadow appears. Marlow is neutral, and colourless like British colonialism. Kurtz is white, as white as ivory, a white obtained by mixing and concentrating all the colours of the spectrum, a white which in a decomposed state is refracted on the gaudy clothes of the young Russian. This motley harlequin is the ultimate mask behind which Kurtz tries to hide, the last folding screen masking his guilt. His last pretext as well, perhaps? Like a molten sun that has set but whose last sparks still linger in the afterglow, Kurtz shines in the rainbow-coloured clothes of his disciple. Is the sun setting in the West? We can understand the significance of the young Russian only in his relationship to Kurtz, just as in *Lord Jim* we understand Jim through Stein. In *Lord Jim*, we remember, Marlow goes to consult Stein, the retired German trader who speaks of his romantic past and his epic combat in the heart of the Malay forest. Stein, a lifeless stone and not a living stone, tells Marlow of the episode when, having killed two Malay bandits, he set off in frantic pursuit of a marvellous, brilliantly coloured butterfly which, ironically, had landed on the forehead of one of his victims. A coloured butterfly in the light of the rising sun.[8] Then, too, the young explorer brings back memories of former glory which haunt the chrysalis, the larva, that goes by the name of Kurtz. It is a striking comparison, that of an explorer at the dawn of his career with another who has lived the last stage of his metamorphosis. Marlow senses this comparison intuitively but cannot completely explain it. Next to this lord of evil, the young harlequin seems to be a kind of altar boy, but that is only an illusion. He is a stand-in for Kurtz in this play. He represents the other side of him. The young harlequin misleads us because he represents a carefree image of rising colonialism, of an operetta-like colonialism, a character who, like the Nanki Poo of Gilbert and Sullivan, survives on adventure – and fresh water – 'A wandering minstrel I . . . ' In reality he is a symbol dressed in bright coloured Holland broadcloth. There is nothing profound about him, but he is certainly more than a figure of pantomime. He is a flat character, but that does not prevent him from being a symbol of colonial expansion. While Kurtz seems to embody all the evils of colonialism, the harlequin proffers his tunic of geographic maps, his toga of pretexts. While Kurtz represents the end-product of colonialism, the young explorer represents its beginnings. In fact, we are closer to Shakespeare here than to an operetta. The relationship between Kurtz and his disciple resembles the one of king and motley. Kurtz, the King Lear of the jungle.

6 Short-Cuts

'Kurtz – Kurtz – that means short in German – don't it? Well, the name was as true as everything else in his life – and death. He looked at least seven feet long.' ('Heart of Darkness', p. 134)

When Marlow makes his discovery, it is the last in a series of startling discoveries. The shrunken heads that he saw grimacing on their stakes like so many parodies of the national flag have brought him crashing down to earth from the height of the edifice which he had constructed piece by piece from each bit of information about Kurtz. Of course he had had the help of reliable people like the young agent at the Inner Station who liked to spread rumours instead of doing their job: 'The business intrusted to this fellow was the making of bricks – so I had been informed, but there wasn't a fragment of a brick anywhere in the station, and he had been there more than a year – waiting. It seems he could not make bricks without something, I don't know what – straw may be.[1] All these straw men are the ones who have built a reputation for Kurtz, about his prowess and his ivory gestures, which goes from mouth to mouth and ear to ear. 'Heart of Darkness' murmurs like a long forest gallery, like an immense whispering gallery. In the shadows behind the colonnades of trees are silhouetted the buildings of the City, all sepulchres, burial vaults and other nefs like St Paul's and Westminster Abbey, murmuring with a rumour of glory and rustling with the pages of the book of honour. Westminster Abbey where Livingstone, the corner stone of the colonial empire in Africa, can permit himself a statue's smile: 'He can smile without bitterness when he remembers the fatal error which put an end to his career as an explorer'.[2]

As for Marlow, he does not have either the excuse or the advantageous point of view of eternity which would permit him to smile. Unlike Livingstone, who dies in a delirium talking about a river, he is the contemporary of his own disappointment. That is why we must consider his remark concerning the real height of Kurtz as more than a banal description, as more than one more element of this portrait. All the distance which separates illusion from reality, the paradox on which the book is constructed, is measured here. Like Lord Jim, whose height is the first thing we learn about him, 'He was just short of six feet', this reference indicates the fundamental inadequacy of the man for the role of hero. Kurtz appears in the full measure of his contradictions. His name is disproportionate to his height. If, as in the case of Jim, we knew from the start that the character lacked the extra inch or so which would have given him a hero's stature, we have to wait until the end of Marlow's voyage to learn the truth about Kurtz. At least that is the way things look on the surface. An attentive reading of the text will show us that the difference between illusion and reality is indicated indirectly in the text from beginning to end. Disguises and masks again! In this sense, Kurtz can be considered not only as the final stage in the journey but as its guiding principle, as its soul. In order to find Kurtz, Marlow will have to follow all the detours of the reputation of Kurtz and wind through the labyrinth of glory which has been erected around Kurtz, just as he follows the innumerable bends of the Congo – which could be compared to the canals of the inner ear. When Marlow arrives within sight of Kurtz, the web spun by the ivory grubber is discovered and disintegrates suddenly. The story, like the *Nellie* riding at anchor and shifting its position with the new tide, changes direction abruptly. On the surface of the story, we have detour which leads to a reversal, and just as Marlow's path will be full of obstacles such as reefs hidden by the current, fog on the river and arrows shot by invisible warriors, the story will include a series of cleverly constructed traps of netting woven, like the story, with a rather broad stitch. At each moment, with each word, the thread of the story risks being cut, either by the intervention of the narrator who could reveal how the story ends before finishing it, or more subtly, by the interventions of the author, who places these netted traps under the very feet of his narrator. There is a constant risk of short-circuiting the story, which is cut short like its model Kurtz and which finds in Kurtz its double-measure.

THE SHORT CIRCUIT OF HUMOUR

Conrad's works are not usually considered to be particularly humorous. On the contrary, one of the criticisms most often implicitly made concerning them is the apparent lack of detachment of a style that is too intense and which, in imposing meaning on the words, excludes automatically the possibility of relaxing tension and releasing humour. In comparison with Fielding or Dickens, Conrad passes for a master craftsman of prose technique. Those of his contemporaries who were close to him emphasised the solemn side of his character which, according to them, was not at all English. Consequently his works were presented as exact reflections of their author, perpetuating a traditional and quite inaccurate idea about books and authors. In the criticism of H. G. Wells, we find this double condemnation: 'The word humour always put Conrad ill at ease. It was one of our Englishisms that he was never able to master.'[3] It is ironic that Wells, a 'progressive' writer in his time who was considered to be a critic of Victorian values, became a defender of pure British traditions where Conrad was concerned. We can easily understand how much arrogance and scorn for another culture are represented by these short lines and we can better appreciate the efforts of the critic F. R. Leavis to reintegrate Conrad (and D. H. Lawrence) into the great tradition of English literature. He delivered both men from the quarantine where they had been confined and gave Conrad a hand over the Channel – of humour. He merits our honest applause. On the other hand, however, Leavis waged his rehabilitation effort in the name of moral values, perpetuating in Conrad's case the very misunderstanding he was trying to eliminate. Conrad's humour is not spectacular but discreet. We would very much like to speak of 'white' humour as in 'white writing', if such humour were not already called 'black'. We could say that in 'Heart of Darkness' white and black go together. What changes our sense of perspective and distracts our attention from the humour is the voice of the narrator Marlow, with whom the story has been all too often identified.

Now Marlow, a man of experience and sound common sense, has only a quite ordinary, limited sense of humour which is accessible to the average reader and profoundly marked by certain gnomic quality. At times, he likes to prod his listeners, whom he finds too sleepy or too conservative, with a remark such as this one: 'I felt often its mysterious stillness watching me at my monkey tricks, just as it watches you fellows performing on your respective tight-ropes for – what is it? half-a crown a tumble – try to be civil, Marlow, growled a voice.'

But we must beware of Marlow, who is no more than a voice and who, as such, is not really much more reliable than Kurtz, for whom he is an echo. A sly kind of humour can be detected in his voice although Marlow's attempts at humour are rather heavy, redundant, and in need of a few more adjectives. His voice is hesitant, trembling from its own vibrations, as if it were subject to doubts about its own existence. Like the pattern which unfolds slowly on the weaver's loom, a certain kind of humour is concealed in the folds of the writing, a kind of humour whose pointed edge rends the text more surely and more profoundly than the long pauses of the narrator. It is rapid, darting humour which short-circuits the text. Thus, inside the very paradox of which Marlow speaks and which is in itself a humorous presentation, is hidden, subconsciously, an invisible subtle humour: 'Well, if a lot of mysterious niggers armed with all kinds of fearful weapons suddenly took to travelling on the road between Deal and Gravesend, catching the yokels right and left . . .' It is not necessary to go further. The destination of the felicitous band is sufficiently clear in itself to show us the way and reveal the pattern. To have these mysterious niggers' land at Deal just as Caesar did is one thing but to put Gravesend on their itinerary is quite another. If Deal and Gravesend are separated on the map by a good fifty miles, it is significant that these two words, by their etymology, are really much closer: they are related like the white wood of the pine tree (deal) and its logical destination as a coffin or a tomb (graves, end) are related. As a slang term, deal can also refer to shady business dealings, a reference which brings the English commercial system directly into the African context, to a continent which it has exploited mercilessly and brought to the brink of ruin. This example of geographical short-circuiting shows us one way in which the text uses symbols like these in its perpetual questioning of itself. This literary introspection brings with it, of course, the risk of extinction. As the narration progresses, the voice of Marlow becomes more and more hesitant, as if he felt he were on the brink of an abyss. As he reacts to his sordid discoveries, he protects himself with what can only be called black humour. It is swift and rapid, which according to Freud's definition of humour, represents a form of economy. The text of 'Heart Darkness' makes such an economical use of words that it barely manages to survive and seems to be constantly on the verge of being engulfed, like the attentive listeners by the night. Here is an example of it. Marlow demands ingenuously of his listeners: 'Light came out of this river since – you say Knights? Yes, but it is like a running blaze on a plain, like a flash of lightning in the clouds.' Two things are evident in this passage. First of all, Marlow is not really responsible for this humour, for he is not conscious of it, since, like a careful, meticulous photographer, he develops this negative into a magnificent coloured print; and secondly, the text is contracted here into its smallest possible unit of existence and plays on the ambiguity of only one word (knight/night). With one single word Conrad is able to play on the opposite colours of black and white, on the whiteness of Galahad and on the blackness of the everlasting night. We could multiply the number of examples where words are used economically and compile a linguistic table that would have nothing round about it at all but which would prove to what extent Conrad was able to develop his poetic faculty in this text by continually measuring with painstaking exactitude the evolution of his ideas and exploiting all the possible meanings of each word. He creates emblems which blot out certain portions of the text and lead the reader from the detours back to the mainstream of the narration. We shall come back to our analysis of these basic structural elements of the text, to words which are exploited to the utmost because these microcosms of the text are paradoxically at the origin of its expansion.

THE ALLEGORICAL SHORT-CUT

In comparison with these basic units which are miniaturised versions of the text, allegorical emblems expand the text, but should still be considered as short-cuts in the narration because they take us rapidly to new meanings which, on the main road of the narration, would have taken much longer to reach. We spoke of humorous short-cuts when the text questioned its authenticity, was contracted and condensed to the utmost and when it remembered its origin humbly, in all modesty. There are humorous short-cuts when a clever genie, the author, pulls the carpet out from under the feet of his witch doctor and poet, Marlow. But if the text receives new impetus from these bursts of humour, it becomes self-explanatory when allegorical symbols are used. The allegorical symbols have a double function that is both dramatic and critical. Take for example the painting done by Kurtz which Marlow notices in the hut of an employee at the Inner Station:

> Then I noticed a small sketch in oils, on a panel, representing a woman, draped and blindfolded, carrying a lighted torch. The

background was sombre – almost black. The movement of the
woman was stately, and the effect of the torch-light on the face
was sinister. (p. 79)

Let us look first at the dramatic function. The painting is associated
with the present time of the narration and has a puzzling aspect
which intrigues Marlow, who makes inquiries of the agent and
discovers that it was painted by Kurtz. Thus painting which gives
Marlow new insight into the personality of Kurtz, is one more sign
marking the road along the quest, and has its place on the list of
symbols of the same type, such as the *Inquiry into some Points of
Seamanship*, but the painting has a retrospective significance as well
as a prospective one. And this is where the critical function of the
symbols takes over. With the blindfold over her eyes and the lighted
torch, this woman whom the painter has arrested in her action
seems to represent all the female characters in the story who, like
sacred statues, have something of her immobility and her ritual
solemnity. We do not suggest that you include on this list either
Marlow's aunt or the two women knitting in the Company's office
in Brussels, but the fiancée of Kurtz and his African mistress are
both fairly well stereotyped in this painting. We encounter the same
blind cult of devotion on the part of the civilised Western woman
and of the primitive African one for this hollow idol Kurtz. For
Conrad, women have the same role to play in the colonial drama,
no matter what side of the conquest they belong to. However, in
their case they are only accomplices and there are extenuating
circumstances. Their very dependence on men means that they are
cut off from their activities and can only learn about their actions by
hearsay, after receiving information which is always presented to
them in its best possible light. They are responsible to the extent that
in their cult of devotion they are like the men who bow down before
ivory and silver or other rare substances. In this respect Conrad's
attitude towards the women of the Victorian era – which, by the
way, would bear some careful examination – should be
reconsidered. His criticism by omission does not represent indifference or hostility: he seems to recognise that their dependency
on men prevents them from learning the truth and making sound
judgements. The painting is an ideological symbol which parodies a
visual form of expression that was in vogue at the time, 'the torch of
progress'. One bears in mind the opening lines of the story which
described the great knight-errants of the sea, those travelling

salesmen of the British kingdom setting out on the avenue of the Thames. Even at the beginning of the story, the sword and the torch cast a shadow on the scene: 'They had all gone out on that sea bearing the sword, and often the torch.' With Marlow, who is more of a realist and more down to earth, this torch is transformed into a flicker, a savage fire poorly disciplined. It is like a flash of lightning in the clouds in comparison to which the tiny light of mortality seems very small indeed; 'We live in a flicker – may it last as long as the old earth keeps rolling.' In this instance, we have a con-tradictory symbol. Blind Fortune has been given the care of the torch of progress, much as if a moustache had been painted on the Mona Lisa. We have criticism of colonial ideology and of the clichés of its rhetoric. This painting questions the validity of Marlow's quest as well as the colonial adventure. The argument can be reduced to a conflict between night and light and translated by a single word: 'Light came out of this river since – you say Knights?'

THE DRAMATIC SHORT-CUT

The short-cut can be of many different types. Conrad imagines subplots which he does not develop according to traditional models, as counterpoint to the main action, but which he stops short or cuts off once he has made his point. No longer than a few lines, they are simple incidents or parentheses which are opened briefly and then closed again. They mirror the main action, both contracting and deforming it, like the short episode of Fresleven and the black hens which put an untimely end to his mission or the Eldorado Expedition which is a grotesque parody of the quest of Kurtz and Marlow. Here again, the text grimaces as if it were seen in a series of trick mirrors, for the pompous rhetoric of colonialism is parroted in every ring under the Big Top of the Grand Magic Colonial Circus by a troupe of travelling clowns. The Eldorado Expedition is like a sideshow whose name alone reveals some very imprecise geograp-hical notions. The expedition takes place in the wrong century and on the wrong continent. The head of the expedition is a butcher who has decided, on a day of fast, to emigrate.[4]

As Marlow will say later, butchers are real pillars of civilisation: 'Here you all are, each moored with two good addresses, like a hulk with two anchors, a butcher round one corner, a policeman round another . . . ' A butcher is a cannibal who shows some restraint.

What could be more fitting than a butcher as the head of an expedition whose principal claim to fame is that it arrives in sections at its starting point?: 'It came in sections during the next three weeks, each section headed by a donkey carrying a white man in new clothes . . . ' These arrivals distinctly remind us of Bouvard and Pécuchet who bought their agricultural equipment and then moved to the country: 'ils s'achetèrent des instruments horticoles puis un tas de choses qui pourraient peut-être servir.'

The Eldorado Expedition bought out all the stores in Europe before heading into the bush: 'Five such instalments came, with their absurd air of disorderly flight with the loot of innumerable outfit shops and provision stores, that, one would think they were lugging, after a raid, into the wilderness for equitable division.' Note what a marvellous vehicle of heteroclite unpacking this sentence is. The sentence makes enormous efforts, jostling along over the dirt paths and clanking over the rails, carrying a load of cumbersome and contradictory meanings. The expedition is announced in 'five instalments.' According to your point of view, that of literature or of commerce, it could either mean in five chapters or in five instalment payments. The Eldorado Expedition seems torn between the episodes of an adventure story or, more prosaically, buying on the instalment plan. It is a hire-purchase expedition or an authentic Victorian bazaar with its tailored outfits for the perfect colonist, outfits suitable for clowns and other actors. Moreover it seems to be a prototype for our modern safaris. What we can read, not between the lines of the text but on its surface, in letters spelled out as clearly as those of a customs stamp, are the glaring deficiencies of these would-be explorers The word lugging, for example, was chosen in all probability by Conrad for the multiple meanings which it suggests, either a piece of *luggage* or a *slug*, a word which contradicts systematically the extreme rapidity of the word 'raid'. The two words seem to neutralise each other and to form a couple which is powerless. As to the ambiguity of the word 'equitable' and its phonetic association with the noble sport of equitation, it could not underline more clearly than it does the grotesque pretensions of the donkey riders. It is quite evident that the passage is a critical reflection on the text itself. Thus the sectioning of the expedition, like its aimlessness, have repercussions on the rhythm of the sentence and give it a cut up, breathless, repetitive movement. Just as the expedition fails to advance, the sentence comes to a halt and makes a formidable point: 'Instead of rivets there came an invasion, an infliction, a visitation.' Just as the expedition arrives piecemeal, in sections, the sentence is also chopped into sections: 'an invasion' comma, 'an infliction' comma, etc. . . .

The supreme irony stems from the fact that these amateur builders arrive instead of the rivets which Marlow and his Belgian engineer had been waiting for. It is just one more proof of the incoherence of the colonial system and of the economic principles which govern it, from the extraction of raw materials to the manufacturing of finished products and their resale to the country which furnished the raw material in the first place. More symbolically, all of the links in the chain which make up the book are reproduced in this sectioning. Marlow himself is the rivet which was missing and which was needed to assemble all the links of the chain.

Marlow is the one who goes from outpost to outpost, from relay to relay, gathering up in the course of his journey all the scattered fragments of the story. More mobile than the civil servants Carlier and Kayerts in 'An Outpost of Progress', who were simply thrown up on an island of civilisation surrounded by a jungle, Marlow patiently follows his clew of Ariadne and finds his way to the Minotaur. Thanks to Marlow, it will be possible to reunite all the pieces of the colonial puzzle. Although his role, which he plays well in spite of himself, ends there and he does not draw any conclusion from his experiences (it falls upon the reader to do this), Marlow does assemble the text. Marionettes like the butcher of the Eldorado Expedition who bring division and strife would have been incapable of assembling it. So would civil servants like Carlier and Kayerts. In this story the civil servants have been integrated into the puzzle as a whole and play their limited and predetermined role, however. They are part of the great colonial chain and relay the latest information about Kurtz. They live under the spell of Kurtz, whom they consider to be the supreme being of colonial progress, their acknowledged master.

The members of the Eldorado Expedition who attempt to assemble their prefabricated expedition in Africa are doomed to defeat before they start, not because they lack strong character – the chief of the Central Station believes strong character is more of a hindrance than a help in these cases: 'Men who come out here should have no entrails' – but because the world belongs to the pure spirits and the hour is no longer favourable for pigherders like Pizarro[5] or for prodigal sons either. The butchers, those civilised murderers, are too fat and too well fed: 'He carried his short paunch on his fat legs.' Only the mad ones, the Ariels who have no consistence, the immaterial beings who harbour contradictions in their breasts or the people like Kurtz, who have made a full circle, the Prosperos who are becoming Calibans, can adventure into the heart of the forest. The others make a short appearance and then disappear. Thus the dance of the Eldorado Expedition with its grotesque merry-go-round of mules throws a new light on the central aspect of the story, and foreshadows a Messiah of sadness, but it is none the less a prophecy which is cut short and comes to nothing.

THE IDEOLOGICAL SHORT-CUT

Of Marlow, we have said that he was the one who assembled the text, that he put together the different links of the colonial chain which apparently had no relation to one another and for which no one else had seen the connection. In other words, his intervention is really the intervention of a voyeur. He appears to be a spectator who slips on stage without being seen, who listens without being recognised, and who solicits confidences without revealing his point of view. The occasions when Marlow gives proof that he is both invisible and invulnerable are numerous. In the shadow of the blaze which devastates the warehouse full of cotton at the Inner Station he is a silent witness of the grotesque actions of the White men and of their expeditive justice. On another occasion he listens to the half-confidences of an agent whom he qualifies as a 'papier-mâché Mephistopheles'. While trying to rest on the bridge of his steamer, he inadvertently overhears an incriminating conversation between the head of the station and his uncle, the head of the Eldorado Expedition, who both want Kurtz dead. In this masque which celebrates the triumph of colonisation, Marlow, the only character with an objective point of view, wanders about without a mask and forces the other characters to drop theirs. Certain agents believe that his attitude is a kind of disguise, like the one Kurtz has: 'The same people who sent him especially also recommended you. Oh, don't say no. I've my own eyes to trust.' And Marlow can only make the following comment which emphasises his surprise: 'Light dawned upon me.' The entire voyage of Marlow is like a dive with eyes wide open into the heart of the night. It is incorrect to assume that Marlow grasps the full importance of the situation right from the beginning, however.

Marlow does not foresee or even anticipate his discoveries but simply muddles through them. He advances on his quest, in much the same way as he pilots his steamer, without charts, avoiding one shoal after another as he encounters them, not seeing much further than the prow of his steamer. Because Marlow can see the enemy he is, however, more lucid than the pilgrims, who are blinded by fear during the first attack and consequently fire wildly into the bush without producing any effect whatsoever, unless we count the smoke-screen which prevents Marlow from seeing where he is going and which represents a dangerous navigational hazard. Marlow also sees things more clearly than the young Russian explorer, who is blinded by his admiration for Kurtz to the point of forgetting the significance of the shrunken heads on the stakes around the compound.

Marlow's voyage or trial, in the literal sense of the word, produces a formal indictment against Kurtz and against colonialism. Proceeding with the impartiality and the wisdom of a judge, Marlow accumulates more and more evidence without ever handing down a verdict. We should also note that that long preliminary investigation is presented as a conflict between what certain witnesses have *heard* and what Marlow *sees* with his own eyes. He investigates every aspect of the reputation which Kurtz has acquired, a reputation that has been blown up out of proportion. In proving that the reputation of Kurtz is undeserved and that he is a grotesque caricature of what he set out to be, Marlow indicts the glorious colonial enterprise which is also a grotesque caricature of what it was meant to be. It is a case of perjury, for the facts contradict the official version of the story.

Edward Said feels that the text represents a conflict between the eye and the ear, between the oral narration and the vision at the heart of Conrad's writing:[6] 'The aim of Conrad is to make us see, that is to say to transcend the absence of everything except the words so that we may enter into a kingdom of vision situated beyond words.' It does not seems to us, however, that the narration tries to indicate what lies beyond the frontier of words and meaning, making the lifeless and far too precise letter vibrate, somehow, by its presence: 'The presence of the spoken word has the effect of tempering, if not blotting out entirely, the written version.' On the contrary, it seems to us that it is the spoken word which is untrue, the spoken word which creates the *myth* and which is on trial here.

During the entire story, Kurtz is only a voice for which other voices are merely echoes. Some voices are as vicious and as nasty as the one belonging to the young Belgian agent who tries to threaten Marlow. When Marlow repeats the insinuations of the young agent for his listeners, his voice reverberates with the feelings of emptiness and nothingness which he experienced at the time:

> It had become so pitch dark that we listeners could hardly see one another. For a long time already he; sitting apart, had been no more to us than a voice. There was not a word from anybody. The others might have been asleep but I was awake, I listened, I listened, I listened on the watch for the sentence, for the word, that would give me the clue to the vain uneasiness inspired by this narrative that seemed to shape itself without human lips in the heavy night-air of the river.

Marlow echoes Kurtz and all his false statements which come from the heart of the forest and these in turn reverberate to the heart of the great cities of the West, but it is no more than a disembodied voice, 'a narrative that seems to shape itself without human lips', that invites us to turn away from the false prophet and warns us not to succumb to the fascination of the 'straightforward' tale of an ingenious narrator like Marlow. This is an imprecise narration and these are shortsighted words because Marlow himself suffers from shortsightedness: 'Do you see him? Do you see the story? Do you see anything?' We must not make of Marlow the spokesman of the book. We must not identify his words, that is to say the moments when he interrupts his narration to comment upon it and to meditate upon it himself, with those of the author. We must not take Marlow on his word alone. It is in the *silence* of the text that, by reading between the lines, we can *see*. Just as Marlow must fish his way among the various vignettes of the colonial drama, the reader must take care not to succumb to the sirens of the text but must be ready to shift course at any moment to avoid them. His mind must constantly be on the alert and he must be ready to leave the mainstream of the narration, to make detours, to adventure on the less trodden paths in the forest of meaning. Many of the problems of interpretation which arise in treating this text arise from the fact that, even though we have been warned not to do this, because we are always trying to find his sailor's wisdom we never let Conrad leave his ship. In this nutshell of a story, on board this light embarcation of a ship's model scarcely heavier than the paper-boats of Rimbaud on their puddles in the north of France, the most important part of the story is not the centre or the nut, but the outside shell. In other words we must turn away from the story's centre and look at it from the outside in order to understand what it really means. Rather than staying on the main road, we must risk losing our way on the less frequented paths. With anguished insistence, Marlow asks his listeners to look beyond the frontiers of his narration. A little as if he were rebelling against the narrow task which had fallen to him to guide the story to its end, he cries out that he is the story's blind spot and asks his listeners to be his witnesses. For that reason we must analyse the images which Marlow brings out from Africa. We must analyse from angles his 'Impressions d'Afrique' – a 'heap of broken images'. For this purpose we have only the rather coarse thread which holds Marlow's narration but like the thread that was used to sew up the binding of *An Inquiry into Some Points of Seamanship*, it is visible. In the apparent disorder of the story there is a hidden order. When Marlow puts his foot on African soil for the first time and climbs the steep hill toward the Central Station, he finds things in a state of complete disarray; everything is desolate and completely run down. Like Marlow, we could be content to make a note of this and continue on our way, but it would be much wiser to wander among all these run-down buildings – in order to understand why they are uncared for. Like Marlow, we could show amazement in an offhand manner and even indifference. We could hasten our step just as he does: 'I didn't want any more loitering in the shade, and I made haste towards the station', but it would be preferable to read between the lines – why not between the words? Rather than to economise on a moment of reflection, rather than to take the shortest route, it would be more worth while to make a detour. Because he does not tarry, Marlow views the African scene with innocence at first. In climbing towards the group of wooden buildings perched on the heights of the coastal cliffs, which is his first destination, Marlow makes a series of startling discoveries. Several symbolic markers are posted on Marlow's path, which is very similar to other arduous routes, to all the narrow paths taken by heroes in search of a problematical salvation. For the chained slaves whose eyes no longer see anything – 'the eyes stared stonily uphill' – the mountain resembles that of Sisyphus. The way of the cross, this Golgotha, leads towards a summit where Marlow is confronted with the unexpected apparition of an impeccably dressed accountant wearing an immaculate white outfit who is calmly doing a series of multiplications and additions. It is like finding St Peter in front of the entrance to Paradise with his nose in his Book of Accounts. It is a vision of a miracle, but it cannot be real. At the summit, the innocence of Marlow is at its peak. The underlying irony, which is a criticism of the terms used by Marlow, comes from the text itself. Marlow goes so far as to express his admiration for the well-dressed man with his sense of order and cleanliness, which he had managed to preserve in a chaotic universe: 'His starched collars and got up shirt fronts were achievement of character.' If he notes the presence of a dying agent lying on a stretcher in the same room as the imperturbable accountant, he does so objectively without showing the slightest trace of emotion. He notes without comment, like the accountant working on his books, both the moans of the dying man and the rather callous attitude of his well-dressed colleague.

It is up to the reader to conclude that this St Peter of the account books, with his appearance of cleanliness – next to godliness isn't it? – is actually more preoccupied with the letter, or rather the numbers, of the law than with its spirit of charity. Marlow is, we repeat, the invisible witness, the third person, who by his presence gathers up the scattered pieces of the text and, without appearing to do so, gives them symbolic value. When all is said and done, Marlow makes his arduous ascent without undue surprise or mental anguish. Unlike Marlow however, we will find deeper meanings in this text and 'account' for things in a different manner.

First of all, at the foot of the slope Marlow discovers boilers and other objects which were abandoned by the Belgians who had intended at one time to build a railroad. There are miniature railroad cars, and drains as well. The boiler officiates on a square of grass, waiting to enter the action. The car has been overturned; its four wheels are up in the air. The rails are rusted. A competent engineer – that is to say, a man who knows the value of things – Marlow is astounded by the wastefulness. Then he encounters the men – a group of slaves chained together and guarded by one of their own who has been promoted to the rank of foreman. Marlow, with his impartial point of view, comprehends the dramatic aspect of the encounter as well as its slightly ridiculous and grotesque side: 'Black rags were wound round their loins, and the short ends behind waggled to and fro like tails.' The attentive reader who knows how to interpret Marlow's documentary notices immediately that the ragged clothes of the slaves and the rhythmic swinging of the chain which binds them together, 'a chain whose bights swung between them, rhythmically clinking', recreates the ragtime rhythm which had been destroyed. Made for music and rhythm, these natives have been taken away from their culture by the deaf and blind White colonists who are unaware of the discords which they have produced in the name of progress. And since it is a question of music, the White colonists prefer another musical sound, the blasting of dynamite which, as faith can for others, can move mountains. The music of the West, of the masters, the Olympian music excludes the syncopated music of the African culture which is considered to be primitive, savage and barbarous.

Further on, Marlow comes upon a narrow ravine which he compares to a scar. It is a Christian wound which has been inflicted on the side of this Golgotha in the bottom of which lies a pile of drainage pipes which have nothing medical about them at all. Last of all, quite by accident, when he thinks he can rest for a minute and clear his head, he seeks some shade under a clump of trees and discovers a group of black shapes, bodies, human bodies, then human faces: 'I began to distinguish the gleam of the eyes under the trees. Then, glancing down, I saw a face near my hand.' This stark image of a black face at the level of a white hand is a short-cut; is a cinematographic effect worthy of a first-rate director. With the black face ready either for beating or for emancipation, it is the image of slavery. Marlow of course, can dispense neither beating nor emancipation, for he has no power whatsoever. That is why he can only make a symbolic gesture, one taught him by Western culture. Good Samaritan that he is, he offers a ship's biscuit to the closest dying man. Marlow is certainly convinced of the inadequate nature of his gesture but it is quite possible that he does not fully comprehend its incongruity. This biscuit, insignificant as it is, is as blatantly unsuitable for its task as all the other apparatus of colonisation. First of all, it is a sea biscuit, a type of nourishment that is not at all adapted to African appetites. Secondly, it is solid food and, as such, lacks the transparency associated with the fresh water with which the Good Samaritan slaked the thirst of Christ. Because of its proximity to leather (Swede/suede) this solid cannot, even with the adjective 'good', be made more tender. Then, too, it is a viaticum stamped with the insignia of the customs agent, rubber-stamped with the sign of possession: 'my good Swede's ship's biscuits'. Like other European products, its value is estimated not according to its worth or nourishing qualities but according to the number of miles that it has been transported. Last of all, because of its resemblance to a communion Host, it has a symbolic value. Marlow is persuaded that he is only comforting a man in distress, but in reality he is sealing a pact of Communion-submission to European values. It is true that his action is placed in an economic context marked by wastefulness, and the fact that somehow this simple biscuit has been miraculously saved, could never compensate for a general shipwreck. This sea biscuit, a small crumb from the island of Robinson Crusoe could be compared to an ark which has survived the industrial deluge. Is this really innocence? This human gesture on Marlow's part should not lead us to make rash conclusions.

The iconography of the book, which includes a fair amount of traditional Christian imagery, only does so within the context of Western culture as a whole; it is only one mythology among many. Marlow advances to the heart of an essentially cultural landscape, to the centre of a continent whose culture, with few exceptions, has disappeared to make room for the theatre of the West.

Like the African slaves who wear cast-off European rags, the African landscape has been colonised. The slaves have black skins but they wear white masks.[7] Unlike the Christian or mythic hero who, like Virgil or Ulysses, ventures into the underworld, Marlow is only an unsuspecting witness whose function is to reveal the text, and to bring the reader up-to-date on the economic, political, and cultural pronouncements of European colonisation. Let us re-consider Marlow's first impressions of Africa. It is certainly not by chance that from the moment he arrives on the coast his discoveries follow a certain kind of logic in spite of the fact that his wanderings seem to be quite aimless. We should look for the pattern in this apparent disorder. First of all, both material objects and human beings have been abandoned and left for dead. As Marlow proceeds towards the summit in this upside-down hell, on this Golgotha which is measured in stages, he is surprised to discover that men and things have little or no value. Ironically, material objects seem to have more life in them than men do. Take, for example, the fat boiler wallowing on the grass or the railroad car with its legs in the air 'like some dead animal'. To complete the irony, the lifeless slaves advancing up the hill in Indian file (the file which could free them from their fetters) are turned into things.

The dying men discovered by Marlow under a clump of trees

were left at the bottom of the ravine like any other useless object. There is nothing human about their bodies, which are no more than 'bundles of acute angles'. They have become mere geometric forms. Conquered by geography, they have become mere quantities. For the remainder of their lives, they can only expect minimal subsistence – that is to say, they must crawl on the ground like animals, like the poor ghost of a lion crawling on all-fours towards the river to drink.

Emblems of death, these slaves are the very negation of the principles set down by explorers like Livingstone or by statesmen like Palmerston, who intended to substitute the commerce of material goods for the commerce of men and to make slavery disappear.

Marlow's first contact with Africa reveals plainly to the reader to what extent this ideal has been perverted. In Africa, where men are treated like things, men's sense of values has been destroyed. Such are the fruits of the *laissez-faire* policy which inspired colonial expansion. By alternating the presentation of things and men in this passage, Conrad gives us more than a series of images, he makes an ideological commentary. We can speak of understatement and of restraint, of a short-cut which allows us to perceive more rapidly than does Marlow the true nature of things. This rapid succession of images is sufficient to make a case against the entire economic system of the West. What could be more symbolic to end this series of accusations than the image of a young Black man wearing a bit of white worsted around his neck? 'Where did he get it? Was it a badge – an ornament – a charm – a propitiatory act? Was there any idea at all connected with it? It looked startling round his black neck, this bit of white thread from beyond the seas.'

There are those who would say that here again we have a passage where the questions of Marlow vibrate like transcendental music on the frontier between words and what lies beyond them. In our opinion, however, these questions are only a ruse conceived by Conrad to put us on the wrong track: 'Was there any idea connected with it?' And the reader in a hurry who places his confidence in the wisdom of the mediator, in the experience of the narrator who has a diploma in storytelling, answers, 'No!' because the answer has been suggested to him. It is not necessary to go any further; there are the frontiers of the unfathomable which cannot be crossed. The hurried reader puts his trust in Marlow who has seen more of the world than he has been able to see in his home county, but, as usual, this battery of questions is really a kind of smokescreen which hides something from the reader. Like the pilgrims, Marlow fires his political salvoes blindly. This should not impress us unduly because he is only an observer who records his experience but does not draw conclusions from 'one of his inconclusive tales'. Now the right answers, because there are correct answers, are cleverly concealed by Conrad, a skilful craftsman, in the first impressions which Marlow has of the African continent.

When you stop to think about it, isn't there a lot of breath wasted over a little piece of white worsted? Marlow noticed that it was incongruous but it is up to the reader to make his clew of Ariadne out of it. This piece of worsted from 'beyond the seas' is precisely the kind of miraculous product which was supposed to free the Africans from slavery and which was supposed to be the symbol of their emancipation. What has it become if not the sign of their alienation? What has it become if not a binding fetter woven in the textile mills of Manchester or Scotland (do not forget that Livingstone spent his early years in the textile mills of Lanark)? What has it become if not a symbol of a double alienation? This is especially true if, as Marlow invites us to do, we give to this piece of worsted a connotation that is both religious and superstitious. Hadn't the poor slave tied the piece of cloth round his neck voluntarily? Such a gesture should have signalled the beginning of a new life for the man but it led him to his death. The passage is a condemnation of the hypocrisy of capitalism which substitutes the subtle persuasion of the new slavery for the violence of the old. That the native had come to consider the piece of worsted as a fetish is a marvellous reversal of situation. If, instead of choosing worsted (worst/worsted), Conrad had chosen cotton, the latter would have become triangular, a miniature replica of the commerce which brings together linked slaves separated by the Atlantic and enchained by the talent of the English textile workers.

7 Full Circle

When Marlow finishes his story and the book comes to an end, we
have the feeling that we have made a full circle and returned to our
starting point. The only difference is that the window of light which
seemed to open at the edge of the sky on the Thames estuary has
been darkened. Darkness has put out the light. There is no longer
even the ironic image of a resurrection, the West is no longer the
negative of the East found in the poem of Baudelaire. 'Et comme un
long linceul traînant a l'Orient . . . ' Here the night is absolute
without any relief in the landscape, without any marked reliefs to
ease the monotony: 'The offing was barred by a black bank of
clouds, and the tranquil waterway leading to the uttermost ends of
the earth flowed sombre under an overcast sky – seemed to lead into
the heart of an immense darkness.' We can easily understand how a
reader, conquered by so much pessimism, wishes to cling to one last
image, to an ultimate idol which will give him a small ray of hope.
He firmly believes he has found it in Marlow who, once the story is
finished, assumes once again the position of a meditating Buddha in
the heart of the night: 'Marlow ceased, and sat apart, indistinct, and
silent, in the pose of a meditating Buddha.' Is Marlow really the last
hope, the last stronghold for this text without pity? He alone seems
to understand how widespread the chaos is; he alone seems to be
able to close, with his enigmatic smile, the infernal opening of the
abyss. Balancing on the wheel of fortune, leaning against the mizzen
mast, that is to say, right in the centre, as if he were leaning against
the beam of a scale: 'Marlow sat cross-legged right aft, leaning
against the mizzen mast. He had sunken cheeks, a yellow
complexion, a straight back, an ascetic aspect, and with his arms
dropped, the palms of his hands outwards, resembled an idol.' This
image is too beautiful to be real! In other words, beware of this
image, and of this idol. Is it not Marlow himself who, without
realising it, has taught us not to bow down to ideas and idols? Wasn't
Marlow the one who, in the preamble to the story, equated ideology
and idolatry by comparing the devotion of the colonists to their

ideal and the devotion of the natives to their idol? The quest is lined
with broken idols like the Khmer statues which Claude takes from
their bases and carries away with him in Malraux's *The Royal way*[1] –
the painted idol of fortune with the torch of progress in its hand –
the fallen idol of the Victorian woman, prisoner in turn of another
idol, man. Kurtz, like Narcissus, idolises himself. Then there are the
primitive idols of the Black natives who come to admire their
oppressors, who clutch at a tiny bit of white cloth and make a fetish
out of it. Idol of idols, an abstract one made of white gold – ivory –
which, like the ridiculous idol of Chester and Robinson in *Lord Jim*
or the silver of the mine in *Nostromo* is the symbol of a certain
nostalgia for a permanent and perfect substance. And it is thus that
Marlow would escape from the iconoclastic violence which produces tremors in the text. We must question that Oriental wisdom of
his which, as the text will bear witness, includes a great deal of near-
sightedness or ignorance. We know two or three things about truth,
affirms Marlow in *Lord Jim*. It is not enough. Rather than hope to
write a whole philosophy in the short space between the two images
which open and close the text (as if he were opening and closing
parentheses), we can say that Marlow hopes only to set the story on
a new course when he breaks the silence with his remark 'And this
also has been one of the dark places of the earth'. But the text begins
long before the intervention of Marlow. This text is divided in two,
like a forked tongue. Which one can we believe? Essentially,
Marlow is an illusion, an optical and an acoustical one. In Marlow's
case, we would be wise to accept him for what he is, a mask, a classic
figure on a theatre curtain. Marlow's two masks, the comic and the
tragic, are really only one; they are really only ornaments of the
text, a way of indicating that it begins and ends. Marlow is a
narrator who exists only because the text does and who retreats into
his shell when the story is finished. The most essential part of the text
is found between the parentheses, in the detour which unfolds in the
form of an expedition and which comprises the story (we can no
longer say that Marlow *is* the story). In one sense, the spiral of the
narration follows and reproduces the bends of the Congo which
fascinated the narrator when he was young and which also
fascinated Conrad.

   In other words, the story generates its own images and its own
geography. These images short-circuit the story and turn it away,
momentarily, from its proposed end. These incidents, interruptions,
detours and snags threaten at every moment to put an end to the

story. In this sense, the story is always conscious of itself and contains an impressive number of different elements. It goes to a series of different places which are all related to one another but which have been displaced. Rome, Ancient Rome, is London, is Brussels the 'sepulchral city'. The city of the sepulchre is thus Jerusalem; the Thames is the Congo; all the agents are one and the same agent, a typical agent, multiplied indefinitely. It is not Marlow alone but all of these elements which make up the story. As these places are all isolated, the story does not really progress and sometimes it even regresses. Does not Marlow's version of the Roman colonisation undermine the official version of the beginnings of the English Empire? With the exception of the narrator, whose principal function, as we have already indicated, is to connect all the links of the chain and to move from place to place so that all the separate parts of the story intersect, the other characters, the real ones, expand and contract the text. Take Kurtz and his disciple, for example. The harlequin with his coat of motley composed of many threads, with his cloak of adventure to which the politics of all the Western nations have contributed, appears at the end of the chain of mediocre colonial agents, the last of the obscure prophets preparing the way for the messiah/Kurtz. He expands the text with his willingness to go ever deeper into the bush and to follow his adventure. He is not in the least affected by this episode which for other characters marks the end of something in their lives. Just as we read from left to right across a page, he moves about the text in a lateral fashion. With Kurtz, as the name clearly indicates, and contrary to the paradoxical affirmation of the narrator, we reach the opposite pole of the story. He is responsible for all the traps and snares which were laid along the river to make the expedition fail. Kurtz is the short-circuit – the dark truth about him is revealed in its harshest light – who disappoints us all the more because we had such high expectations for him. And it is thus that the colonial conquest unfolds, from day to night and from hope to deception. The first efforts to open the way to the East raised high hopes, but the colonial adventure was soon bogged down in the mud of Africa, in the traps and snares for which the participants were totally unprepared. The story swings back and forth between two poles of attraction, towards the Orient of the fable forever expanding, towards the never-ending series of interlocking tales,[2] but which also contracts towards its premature ending. At this point, we can resurrect Marlow briefly and lend our ears to this indefatigable storyteller –

before immediately cutting him off, by the way – because Marlow, too, with a greater degree of suppleness, enters into this process of expansion and contraction, aware that he has the obligation to speak and to reveal his inmost convictions but realising at the same time that it would be wiser for him to be silent. Marlow's voice rings false in his own ears because he discovered in Africa how empty and inadequate is the language of the West. Marlow listens to himself spinning a yarn whose rather coarse thread is woven of several more subtle threads and is sometimes pulled as tight as a tight-rope.

Part III
Analysis of the West

8 Tribal and Economic Exchanges

> Hurry up, please, it's time'
> T. S. Eliot, *The Waste Land*

In 'Heart of Darkness', the sun was beginning to set on the Empire. In *The Secret Agent*, its final hour has come. The colonial dream has retreated to the metropolis; the last servants of the colonial adventure are gathering dust in the vast necropolis of Whitehall – like so many mummies wrapped in funereal bands: ' "Here I am stuck in a litter of paper," he reflected with unreasonable resentment.' Litter/letter. With the setting sun, the scribes can now recline on Oriental beds. Space, which was still excentric in 'Heart of Darkness', has become homogeneous. In 'Heart of Darkness', the Thames and the Congo, in spite of their similarities, were still distinct from each other, separated in time and space by the time it took Marlow to tell his tale. In the privileged domain of paradox, rigorous logic separated the two elements of the comparison, both to prevent exact identification and to allow the comparison to be made, with the result that one image was superimposed on the other and, at times the reader had the impression of seeing double. Just as Rome had not always been the capital of the world, London had once been no more than a remote Roman suburb. Thus excentricity depended upon the conjunction of centres. It was only a matter of time – of centuries, to be exact – before the Congo would come to resemble the Thames. In 'Heart of Darkness', the illusion of another place, a somewhere else, outside the known and familiar sphere of things, was necessary in order to make the familiar universe which people thought was expanding seem more visible.

In reality, however, the universe was contracting and retracting. In *The Secret Agent*, London, which is haunted by anonymous agents of unknown origin, is a closed and neutral space. Both homes and streets, faithfully reflecting one another in a confined area, are lit by gloomy monotony of gas, a product of decaying matter:

> Down below in the quiet, narrow street measured foot-steps approached the house, then died away, unhurried and firm, as if the passer-by had started to pace out all eternity, from gas-lamp to gas-lamp in a night without end . . . 'Did you turn off the gas downstairs?' 'yes, I did,' answered Mrs. Verloc, conscientiously. (*The Secret Agent*, pp. 57–8)

Undressing for the night, Mr Verloc sees a strange apparition on the dark pane of the bedroom window, a grotesque icon, which is a reminder of the bonds uniting East and West:

> And suddenly the face of Mr. Vladimir, clean-shaved and witty, appeared enhaloed in the glow of its rosy complexion like a sort of pink seal impressed on the fatal darkness. (p. 57)

Mr Verloc resembles the closed, colourless city in which he lives. He is a nobody, a nonentity, who does nothing and goes nowhere, a figure of complete domesticity in the familiar London streets. His lot is not so much the result of indecision as of lack of commitment. His approach to life is neutral and represents the annulment of contrary forces. His name, which, as is fitting for a secret agent, is not memorable, brings together two opposing forces – opening (overture) and closing (lock) – if one is willing to lend an attentive ear. If no suitable key can be found for Verloc's 'lock', his circle of revolutionaries includes Michaelis, a locksmith who was once arrested with a bunch of skeleton keys in his pocket – an unfortunate, ironic coincidence where we must suppose the hand of fate to be at work. Michaelis, the 'ticket-of-leave-apostle' is one of Verloc's multiple doubles whose forces of inertia confirms the general law of gravity in this retracting universe. Even with his 'skeleton' keys this obese revolutionary would be at a loss to live as a free man. The only liberation he can conceive of is a literary one which, ironically, reproduces the conditions of his life in prison:

> Michaelis was writing night and day in a shaky, slanting hand that *Autobiography of a Prisoner* which was to be like a *Book of Revelation* in the history of mankind.

The conditions of confined space, seclusion, and solitude in a small four-roomed cottage were favourable to his inspiration. It was like being in prison, except that one was never disturbed for the odious purpose of taking exercise according to the tyrannical regulations of his old home in the penitentiary. He could not tell whether the sun still shone on the earth or not. The perspiration of the literary labour dropped from his brow. A delightful enthusiasm urged him on. It was the liberation of his inner life, the letting out of his soul into the wide world. (p. 120)

Within the closed, confined space of London, it is no longer possible to think of founding anything. The traditional family epic in which the homeland is forsaken for exile, is ironically parodied in the saga of Winnie Verloc taking her mother to an institution for old people across a desolate urban landscape in 'a metropolitan hackney carriage' with a 'maimed driver on the box'. The rhetoric reaches truly epic heights and time seems to be suspended when the hackney cab passes in front of the Treasury building: time is money, isn't it? 'The rattle and jingle of glass went on indefinitely in front of the long Treasury building – and time itself seemed to stand still'. The clanking carriage, carrying an epic family, a royal family, follows the route of the Jubilee – Queen Victoria in a decrepit coach whose final destination is a Charity Foundation and who will be left to yellow with age in a setting worthy of Dickens:

A range of gabled little houses, each with one dim yellow window, on the ground floor, surrounded the dark open space of a grass plot planted with shrubs and railed off from the patchwork of lights and shadows in the wide road, resounding with the dull rumble of traffic. (p. 165)

In such a monotonous, undifferentiated universe, the only conceivable form of exoticism is of the social order, where prevailing currents are vertical, not horizontal. Take for example, the Assistant Commissioner who leaves the rampart of his social position to dive into the mire of the London underworld: 'His descent into the street was like the descent into a slimy aquarium from which the water had been run off. A murky, gloomy dampness enveloped him.' (p. 147) The social structure of London society could be compared to a triangle in which the illusion of difference could only be achieved when moving vertically from the summit towards the base. If the length of the base measures the distance which separates order from disorder, Chief-Inspector Heat from secret agent Verloc, for example, that separation becomes quite artificial, especially when summit meetings are involved. Ambassadors, theoreticians of anarchy and police inspectors meeting in the drawing-rooms of the aristocracy are eager to maintain cordial relationships and try not to harm one another. When, without warning, this gentleman's agreement is not adhered to by one of the members – as in the case of the Russian Ambassador Vladimir who is exposed by the blunder of Verloc – the supreme punishment is of being excluded from élite society. In Vladimir's case, the exclusion in question is from a so-called 'Explorers' club. When we stop to think about it, Vladimir's forced departure from a club so named is more than a little futile. Locked in the Siberia of his embassy, Mr Vladimir will undergo only a temporary social exile. Moreover, the particular summit from which he falls is only one among many higher ones, representing the true heights of power, where the most important alliances are made. It is the Assistant Commissioner, on the advice of Sir Ethelred, who gains access to the nerve centre of power. He does so by simply going from one floor to another, from home to Home with a capital H – a word big enough to take in the whole earth – to the Home Secretary. In a domestic contest like this one, the concept of something foreign can no longer exist. The outsiders have been colonised to such an extent by the insiders that the expression 'paynim' (foreign) is used as stock insult by the members of the same house, the house *par excellence*, the house of verbal exchanges, the House of Parliament.[1]

That this particular Home Secretary should be interested in fisheries and in their nationalisation – that is to say, their domestication – seems to be no more than a very minor detail whose real import dawns upon us slowly – a bit fishy, isn't it? Do not forget that the Assistant Commissioner had compared London to a vast, slimy aquarium or that the Home Secretary, the executor of imperial power, whose main ambition is to transform all the seas of the globe into a series of communicating basins, is the master of even the smallest fishes in the sea. On a domesticated universe like this one trade is what makes the world go round. Money, which is the sole measure of success or failure and the base of exchanges, is also the source of corruption and of the loss of integrity. Commercial society, too, has a triangular form, a form which distorts the true nature of reality.

Verloc, a fishy, slimy double agent in his dual quality of spy and distributor of pornographic literature is the prototype of figures like Madame Sosostris, Mr Eugenides or Tiresias himself,[2] who are masters of changes and exchanges. The obscene publications hanging in Verloc's shop window, like so much washing out to dry, are cut of the same stuff as the City typist's undergarments in 'The Waste Land'[3]

> Out of the window perilously spread
> Her drying combinations touched by the sun's last rays . . .

The colourless alloy of a monetary unit is at the base of a linguistic triangle as well, one which brings together money, travelling and food. Fare is the price paid for a service; in a wayfarer, it can be the traveller; becoming fare once again, it is a repast. When the words roll on the invisible bearings of multiple meanings, their depths should be plumbed. In Winnie Verloc's own words: 'a simple sentence may hold several diverse meanings'. Take the example of a sentence like the following one: 'Tendering a coin through the trap door, the fare slipped out and away.' Is not the lucre of trade and exchanges the real secret agent, the agent/*argent* of duplication and duplicity, the true prime mover of this closed universe. Like so many customers or fares, are we not taken back along the route already followed by Winnie Verloc's cab, which threaded its way between time and money? The secular trinity that governs the course of the social order, whose emblem, the delta, is worn by Mr Verloc, cannot disguise its commercialism under the appearance of holiness or religion.

Another unit of society which has a triangular structure, the holy Verloc family, is one of the basic cells of imperial society, a force for order and disorder thanks to its apex and axis, Mr Verloc. The Verlocs represent the degeneration of the Christian family in so far as their apparent respectability is only a cover-up for repressed savagery. Could we consider the secret agent to be the third man – a middleman dealing on both sides of the coin? You may wish to call them a degenerate family because of the distance which separates the father from the son, the duplicity of the father from the simplicity of the son. The divorce between power and sensitivity could not be more evident. No matter which way we attempt to turn the coin, we cannot bring both sides together. Is it possible, then, to speak of a rescue by the son, of a redemption by innocence in such a loveless trinity?

> 'This music crept by me upon the waters'
> And along the Strand, up Queen Victoria Street.
> O City city, I can sometimes hear
> Beside a public bar in Lower Thames Street
> The Pleasant whining of a mandoline
> And a clatter and a chatter from within
> Where fishermen lounge at noon.

Fishers of men or urban cannibals, manna from heaven or earthly meat, food and dogma have become stale and tasteless. The route to the Orient, the route of the Crusaders, is hidden by the thick, grey London fog, and even foreign cuisines have lost their exotic flavour in this confined universe:

> On going out the Assistant Commissioner made to himself the observation that the patrons of the place had lost in the frequentation of fraudulent cookery all their national and private characteristics. And this was strange since the Italian restaurant is such a peculiarly British institution. (p. 149)

The loss of national and private characteristics is not only a surface phenomenon in so far as earthly and spiritual nourishment is concerned. In the Christian tradition, breaking bread together was considered to be the continuation of a sacrificial offering. In this novel, a kind of primary cannibalism seems to replace it; the son is sacrificed by an unloving father in a grotesque parody of Judaic drama, Chief-Inspector Heat arrives too late to heat up, to eat up the leftover. After the sacrifice, the head of the family thinks only of restoring his own body with a piece of cold meat and fails to notice the passionate reaction of his wife or her preparations to put an end to his feast. In a new version of the eternal triangle, Winnie Verloc coldly refuses her husband's advances out of respect for Stevie's memory; the father has devoured the son but will be devoured in turn in a domestic outburst of cannibalism. At the Verloc's last supper, the members of the family prey upon one another in a grotesque caricature of Christian sacrifice.

Not even exotic Eastern spices can disguise the tastelessness of Western farce, that seems to be empty of meaning; in the kitchens of Western civilisation, the creative flux has been ground down to nothingness by infernal social and domestic machines. Even the would-be revolutionaries are part of the infernal mechanism. Their inability to dominate the situation is due less to the political tenets which they believe in than to the sense of inertia which they experience in an all confining universe. The three revolutionaries – Michaelis, the Professor and Ossipon – from another triangle, much like the one formed by the Verloc family, and reflect a disorder similar to theirs. The domestic and social order are in turn reflected in the political order, just as the Shadow Cabinet reflects the Cabinet of the Prime Minister. A parody of the various trinities consecrated by Western civilisation, *The Secret Agent* is also a criticism of Hegel's dialectical triad, devised to deal with contradictions. In Conrad's eyes no logic, no theology has the power to redeem matter or to regulate its creative flow. Instead of arriving at a synthesis which takes into account the negative aspects and concluding with the discovery of a new premise, here the dialectical process stops short in what amounts to a tragic annulment of opposing forces. Verloc, himself, who has the rather imposing title of 'Secret Agent' is only the delegate of a shadowy foreign power: 'I want to affirm that Mr Verloc's expression was by no means diabolic' implies in its double negation the insignificance of a man who cannot even claim to be a legitimate heir to that prince of negators, the devil. The metaphysical system on which Western civilisation was based is actually short-circuited by the unremarkable, colourless Verloc. The 'poor devil' moves into the darkness that was still undomesticated in 'Heart of Darkness' and which, with his presence, can no longer remain black but turns to grey. The heroic complicity which united Marlow and Kurtz – the envoy of Christianity and the prince of darkness – has given way to the sordid duplicity of the anonymous double-agent. Michaelis and Verloc are just so many nondescript figures who might have been anything, really. Anything from 'frame-maker to locksmith' could not be more appropriate, for Michaelis is indeed a locksmith by trade and Verloc, although his lock is in name only, has a warped mind. Interchangeable doubles, they bear witness to the neutrality of spaces which are both open (anything) and closed (frames and locks).

Within that neutral space, it is impossible to differ. All the room in it is taken up by the infinite reproduction of the basic triangle, the family. Only the mad Professor, a maker of explosives, tries to escape the gravity of his fate, which confines him to the closed urban sphere. He wanders about London as if on the brink of a precipice, a quietly disquieting figure, ready at any moment to set off an india-rubber device in his pocket to send him – and many others – to a kind of collective doom. In the mad Professor, the quest for origins has found, logically enough, a suitable realm in the domain of death. The Professor's position, which Ossipon describes as being transcendental, is the perfect example of idealism trying to base its power on negativity. The Professor prepares his retreat in the immortal realm of death and acquires a strange kind of mastery over time – which assimilates him, temporarily, with the gods. For the Professor, the only possible means of differentiating oneself from the mass of humanity is to have the power to hasten or delay the moment of death and to be in constant command of that negative power. Such power is not only negative but severely limited as well, in as much as it is destined to remain always latent. Like Mallarmé's Prince Hamlet the Professor will never come to power. He cannot incarnate himself without being disincarnated, without losing the essence of his being. His loathing for matter, mankind and their eternal reproduction transforms his exotic conception of death into a model of domesticity. What this stifling world is looking for, condemned as it is to die 'not with a bang but a whimper',[4] is, to be precise, a way out. Even Stevie, stumbling with a bomb against a root at Greenwich, is not an exception to the rule. His fall proves how powerful the law of gravity is in a retracting universe. His body, transformed into a pathetic heap of nothingness, will eventually, metaphorically, feed Verloc's ravenous appetite – Verloc, his adoptive father. Stevie does not offer the slightest hope of salvation to the world which destroyed him, however. He will serve as one more link in the food chain but all spiritual communion is impossible. In devouring its sons, time devours itself and is reproduced in its fall. There is no point here in attempting to plunge into the heart of the matter, with St Anthony.[5] Space is exoticism, writing landscape, and music is where time, as if hypnotised, is forgotten. With the closing of space, with the closing of the gate at the first meridian in Greenwich Park, the park of the Fall, the mirage of origins recedes for ever. For Flaubert, Carthage was like a stage; for Michel Foucault, theory is a welter of cleverly designed planes, unfolded on a series of stages.[6] Space rends the nakedness of time and Conrad is not prepared to clothe, even with tears, even with death, that eternal nakedness.

9 Mining and Refining Reality

Nostromo has been described as a summit in Conrad's work. It is possible to take that remark literally and consider that a sense of descriptive geography, an interest in continental reality, replaces here the more fluid elements of the earlier novels. Even the faults resulting from the plications of stratified chronology take on a crystallised, solidified, spatial perspective.

The apparent massiveness of the work, the apparent reconstruction of a real world, is actually full of fissures and faults – like the mountainside where the mine is located – which are the direct result of the mining operations. It seems to us that the mining activity around which the fiction is conceived, and which leaves an indelible imprint on the novel's form, is essential to our understanding of the book as a whole. Like the very refining process which it describes so well, the writing splits the text to extract the ore which will be transformed into the precious metal of fiction.

As readers we should try to put aside any preconceived linguistic or psychoanalytic theories we may have, imagine the different steps in its creative process and reflect upon them in order to discover exactly what is entailed.

CONTRACTION

The town of Sulaco, a coastal port of the imaginary Republic of Costaguana, is remarkable for its inaccessibility. It can only be reached after a long sea voyage or after crossing a high cordillera which is frequented almost exclusively by the most zealous of businessmen or the most desperate of bandits.

Sulaco, a South American replica of an Oriental setting like Berau, where men like Almayer or Willems slowly lose their illusions about life, bears the unmistakable Conradian stamp of isolation.

In *Nostromo*, however, the geographical site is less a symbolic place or a spiritual borderland suited to an excess of wasted romance than a battleground where ideologies are pitted against one another.

Just because so many critics have locked Conrad in a maritime prison, we must not think that this space is neutral or that any space could ever be neutral for Conrad. He uses the geography of Sulaco strategically, as a military expert would. He has taken sides and chooses his place of battle carefully.

A series of fortresses dot the 'discontinuous' landscape of romance. The vulnerable fortress of the liberal innkeeper Giorgio Viola is located on the outskirts of the town, outside the wall, where he remains entrenched in the midst of the dangers of the revolution. Then there are the respective fortresses of the conservative elements, the homes of Charles Gould and diplomat Don José Avellanos, which face each other. We must not forget the natural and economic fortress of the mine where feudal alliances between the native workers, the Roman church, the governor of the mine and the bandit Hernandez will be contracted in the name of local interest. Lastly, there is the Customs fortress, where Captain Mitchell, Marlow's distant kin, blindly refuses to see any other point of view than his own.

Instead of being forgotten by the rest of the inhabitants of the earth as Patusan was, Sulaco is constantly threatened by economic and military invasions. Here the world of romance is subject to revolutionary anarchy and capitalistic logic (and logistics), both of which, contrary to appearances, have the same effect. The makers of revolution are responsible for the contraction of bodies and souls under torture (Dr Monygham and Hirsch, the Jewish merchant); the capitalists, who are masters of linear technology, firmly believe they have the power to stretch space to its utmost limits and attempt to put an end to Sulaco's isolation by constructing a railway.

So it happens that the isolation of a feudal society like Sulaco is slowly transformed, under the impulsion of political and economic conflicts, into a satellite of the empire of the Californian financier Holroyd, (a kind of nineteenth-century Howard Hughes) 'In the great Holroyd building (an enormous pile of iron, glass, and blocks of stone at the corner of two streets cobwebbed aloft by the radiation of telegraph wires) . . .' (*Nostromo*, p. 80)

SEDIMENT

Nostromo, a book without any depth to it. The warning from 'Heart of Darkness' that the meaning of an episode does not always lie within can also apply here: 'and to him the meaning of an episode was not inside like a kernel but outside, enveloping the tale which brought it out only as a glow brings out a haze.' In *Nostromo* we leave behind the varied points of view which give *Lord Jim* its illusion of depth, as well as the use of myth which confers an air of profundity to 'Heart of Darkness'. Instead, Conrad chooses in *Nostromo* to paint a series of miniatures, portraits and large frescoes on many different surfaces, much as Flaubert did in *Salam—bô*.

In *Nostromo*, the frescoes deal with history. The story is interrupted momentarily so that a vast panorama of historic detail can be presented. In captain Mitchell's words, these frescoes taken from the pages of time usher in a new era. It is not surprising that the frescoes depicting a feudal world are mostly equestrian. There is the escort for the first consignment of silver, which is portrayed galloping down the slopes of the mountain to the harbour, led by the mounted figure of Don Carlos. There is the cavalry detachment commanded by General Barrios which embarks upon the lighters of the Company to go and fight Montero in the north. There is the population of Sulaco fleeing before the arrival of 200 revolutionaries on horseback.

Very often the portraits mark the entrance of a character in the narrative. Sometimes the portrait takes the form of a simple caricature. When a character is flattened out in such a way, we may infer that his rank in the narrative hierarchy is not high. Such is the case of a soldier like General Montero:

> The white plume, the coppery tint of his broad face, the blue-black of the moustaches under the curved beak, the mass of gold on sleeves and breast, the high shining boots with enormous spurs, the working nostrils, the imbecile and domineering stare of the glorious victor of Rio Seco had in them something ominous and incredible; the exaggeration of a cruel caricature, the fatuity of solemn masquerading, the atrocious grotesqueness of some military idol of Aztec conception and European bedecking, awaiting the homage of worshippers. (p. 122)

The narrative follows a rhythm of its own and, in alternating between portraits and frescoes, makes an entirely new use of space.

Each portrait is part of a larger fresco which ensures that there is a certain amount of reciprocity between the two modes. In the fresco of the first convoy taking the silver ingots to Sulaco, Conrad includes the detail of Doña Emilia Gould waving to her husband from a balcony. Conversely, when Conrad paints the portrait of Nostromo on horseback going to the arena, he includes in the background some of the cavalcades and epic rides which will take place in the novel.

We will not speak of depth as such in this novel but of sediment, of the residue of the mining process. And we will need very sharp eyes indeed not to be fooled by the many different shining surfaces. Instead of depth, we have complexity and a vast array of details which blind even the most perceptive of the characters in the novel. There is the vast amount of human detail which baffles Don Pepe and Father Roman when they try to identify the younger members of their flock:

> And it was not only the men that Don Pepe knew so well, but he seemed able, with one attentive, thoughtful glance, to classify each woman, girl, or growing youth of his domain. It was only the small fry that puzzled him sometimes. He and the padre could be seen frequently side by side, meditative and gazing across the street of a village at a lot of sedate brown children, trying to sort them out, as it were, in low consulting tones, or else they would together put searching questions as to the parentage of some small, staid urchin (p. 102)

Such a desire for complexity is ambiguous and seems here to achieve a degree of completeness matched only by a well-kept police file. Yet, as a contrast to the exhaustiveness of Don Pepe and Father Roman, there is Mrs Gould's patent unability to differentiate the Indians' faces, which all look the same to her. In this sense, Mrs Gould shares naïvely in the colonial blindness of refined Europeans:

> He could distinguish them not only by their flat faces, which to Mrs. Gould looked all alike, as if run into the same ancestral mould of suffering and patience, but apparently also by the infinitely graduated shades of reddish-brown, of blackish-brown, of coppery brownbacks, as the two shifts, stripped to linen drawers and leather skull-caps, mingled together with a confusion of naked limbs, of shouldered picks, swinging lamps, in a

great shuffle of sandalled feet on the open plateau before the entrance on the main tunnel. (p. 100)

As for the desire of Don Pepe to get to the bottom of things, it should be taken for what it is: he exploits in depth the human material, the Indian population, and remembers every one of them down to the last detail of the carboniferous and coloured stratification of their backs.

FRAMES

Let us change our perspective for a moment and try to look at things from the vantage point of the point of view. In *Lord Jim* the centre's preservation was ensured by the continuing existence of a reservation far from the centre – by excentricity itself. In 'Heart of Darkness' Kurtz's world could no longer be considered excentric when Africa became a suburb of London. In *Nostromo* excentricity is no longer possible, for centralisation is everywhere.

Everything is seen inside one single frame which can be taken in at a glance by the eye; it is a visual universe, of course. This is part of Conrad's programme, we know: to make us see. In *Nostromo*, secrets are only secrets in so far as they have yet not come to light or been extorted by torture.

Each narrative unit revolves on the axis of a viewpoint, of someone who sees. At times, the narrative, in seeming contradiction with the logical sequence of events, opens on new vistas. Sometimes it opens a door which could have remained closed, as when Giorgio Viola is barricaded with his family in the inn, during the uprising:

It had only one window, and its only door swung out upon the track of thick dust fenced by aloe hedges between the harbour and the town, where clumsy carts used to creak along behind slow yokes of oxen guided by boys on horseback. (p. 18)

Through this loophole in the text, a kind of hidden camera makes a wide-angle, panoramic shot that takes in historical and geographical information and gives a new dimension to the intrigue.

Some characters in the novel seem to have the privilege or right to see, which they use in either an ethical or an aesthetic domain. Decoud and Mrs Gould are two of these characters. Mrs Gould owes her fondness for drawing to her European background.

Extremely sensitive to the passive nature of things, she captures in a vivid watercolour the majesty of a waterfall which had to be diverted in order for the mine to be exploited and which will exist no more:

> Only the memory of the waterfall, with its amazing fernery, like a hanging garden above the rocks of the gorge, was preserved in Mrs. Gould's water-colour sketch; she had made it hastily one day from a cleared patch in the bushes, sitting in the shade of a roof of straw erected for her on three rough poles under Don Pepe's direction. (p. 106)

In Conrad's description of the painting of Mrs Gould's watercolour (a watercolour for a waterfall) the artist's intention is less important than the conditions under which it was painted. The aesthetic eye was controlled by the overseer Don Pepe who supervised the material preparations for installing Mrs Gould. In a sense, the arts are patronised by the economic eye of industry. Elsewhere in the novel, Holroyd's sisters-in-law travel across Europe making sketches of medieval villages:

> A few months before he had made his acquaintance in a old historic German town, situated in a mining district. The American had his womankind with him, but seemed lonely while they were sketching all day long the old doorways and the turreted corners of the medieval houses. (pp. 64–5)

With so many people drawing, and sketching from so many different points of view, no one eye alone can claim to control *Nostromo* and guide its destiny. Different points of view not only overlap but also obliterate one another. Some remain totally distinct from one another. So, then, what about an omniscient look? Should we conclude that in *Nostromo* Conrad attempts to describe phenomenologically the relation of different individuals to truth and reality?

PROCESS

Nostromo is a novel of transition, both in Conrad's own work and in the development of the British novel in general. In *Nostromo*,

Conrad discovers new veins in the mine of fiction which he cannot exploit fully but which will soon be exploited by others. Virginia Woolf would be one of those who would capitalise on Conrad's rich lode, in *To the Lighthouse*, essentially.[1] D. H. Lawrence exploits another vein with his pondering on the nature of man's relationship to the land, both agrarian and industrial; or to the Indian lands, since Mrs Gould is bound to ride away some day by herself and offer herself to some sacrificial Indian knife.[2] But, as we have already seen in our study of 'Heart of Darkness' and 'Lord Jim', Conrad prefers to follow the difficult path along the great divide of fiction, along the line of faults and imperfections.

In one sense, seeing is overemphasised in *Nostromo* and far too much importance is given to the eye, as if writing seemed to question itself incessantly and to feel itself extorting truth from reality. In this respect Conrad's decision to use frescoes and portraits in well-defined frames is related to the centralisation of the state of Sulaco caused by progressive industrialisation.

Western logic, based as it is on cause and effect, can be described as linear. Because this form of reasoning is eager to contract space, depth and volume, reality is distorted. A certain theatricality – we might even say a certain militarisation, whose theatres of operation are the mine, the palace, the parliament, the arena and the square – inevitably appears.

The crux of the problem treated in *Nostromo* is no longer the alienation of the individual consciousness. Depth is achieved in the portrayal of a complex society whose metamorphoses are not evaluated in religious terms. In short, Conrad does not attempt to sound human depths but chooses to overlap many different perspectives of human activity.

Unlike Lawrence, Conrad does not believe in a restoration of the Indian bond in modern society. Mythology functions intermittently and without much success in *Nostromo*. A few coastal vessels bear the names of devalued Olympian divinities, like the *Juno*, the *Ganymede*, the *Cerberus*, and the only native divinities to be found in the entire book are the ghosts of the two gringos whom the mountains swallowed up after their lust for gold led them astray.

As to Mrs Gould's 'Indianism' which is so strikingly prophetic of D. H. Lawrence's and is based, like his, upon Mediterranean sources – 'Having acquired in Southern Europe a knowledge of true peasantry, she was able to appreciate the great worth of the people. She saw the man under the silent sad-eyed beast of burden'

—Conrad leaves little doubt as to its nostalgic, even exotic nature, accessible only to the sensibility of Europeanised souls.

We can add here that the Indian revolution of the brother of General Montero, Pedro, who grew up on a diet of European fiction, rapidly becomes a dictatorship that is a forerunner of those set up by the fascist leaders of modern times:

> On his left hand, Gamacho, big and hot, wiping his hairy wet face, uncovered a set of yellow fangs in a grin of stupid hilarity. On his right, Senor Fuentes, small and lean, looked on with compressed lips. The crowd stared literally open-mouthed and in eager stillness, as though they had expected the great *guerillero*, the famous Pedrito, to begin scattering at once some sort of visible largesse. What he began was a speech. He began it with the shouted words 'Citizens!' which reached even those in the middle of the Plaza. Afterwards the greater part of the citizens remained fascinated by the orator's action alone, his tip-toeing, the arms flung above his head with the fists clenched, a hand laid flat upon the heart, the silver gleam of rolling eyes, the sweeping, pointing, embracing gestures, a hand laid familiarly on Gamacho's shoulder, a hand waved formally towards the little black-coated person of Senor Fuentes, advocate and politician and a true friend of the people. (pp. 389–90)

It is easy to understand why there is no room for myths in *Nostromo*. No room for myths perhaps, but what about metaphor? We believe that the text functions as a metaphor of itself, that the fictional process corresponds to the refining activity which the mining ore undergoes.

There are two principal operations in the refining process of silver ore, the passage of the ore through the shoots and its subsequent transformation under the stamps. 'There was no mistaking the growling mutter of the mountain pouring its stream of treasure under the stamps' (note the monetary value of the word stamps). The transforming process, the presence in the story of shoots and stamps, assures the continued circulation of historic and economic truths.

Once the ore is transformed into silver, the circulating process is endlessly accelerated. Loaded on a lighter in the harbour (note the irony of the word lighter, which will prove to be a craft far too light for such a load), the precious metal is sent to San Francisco and returns to Sulaco in the form of investments, railway investments, for instance, which are destined to make transportation of all kinds more rapid and more efficient – so that the shoots and stamps will be fed all the more rapidly and their product sent into the financial circuit with even greater swiftness.

Along the route of the silver are found men and women who, with varying degrees of involvement in the process, will cling to the illusion of their own independence. The time has come to speak of Nostromo. He is an absentee hero who, like the flashing beam of a lighthouse, is seen only intermittently. It is up to the other characters in the story to spread his fame abroad (like Kurtz).

In spite of his splendid isolation, Nostromo is one of the most effective agents of the centralising process. Like Kurtz, he identifies himself so completely with the industrial process that his own personality seems to get lost in the shuffle. The loss of his individuality makes of him less of a real person and more of an image of the forces at work in Sulaco.

FRACTURES

Ironically enough, Nostromo's heroic awakening after losing the lighter, his appearance at the centre of the intrigue of the novel, coincides with his social eclipse and the beginning of a discreet life of criminal activity. On his awakening, Nostromo discovers how powerful money really is and also the nature of the role he was being made to play in the money game. The new light shed on the subject by his conversation with Dr Monygham is symbolised by the image of the lighthouse (which lights the bay where the lighter floundered). Ironically, Nostromo believes that the lighthouse no longer holds any danger for him because he has put his friends the Violas in charge of it.

Lighthouse/lookout: through the lighthouse, through the eyes of Nostromo, watching, the silver is constantly, symbolically visible. Indication/indicator.

The individual conscience – like the lighthouse a symbol of isolation – is perhaps an unhappy conscience. It is none the less true that the individual action of Nostromo is Promethean – theft of silver, theft of fire, theft of light – and also directly related to his revolt against the commercial exchanges of the community. That is why we must not minimise the importance of what he does by measuring it against a kind of ethical silver standard which depreciates the value of isolation: it is through Nostromo's revolt alone that tragedy enters the story.

Yet, his heroism seems to point to something far beyond him. By his theft, Nostromo does not merely revolt against the visible idol of money and put himself outside the circuit of economic exchanges to which he was so intimately associated. On denying what determined him, he affirms the power of determination at the same time. We cannot not define something. Nor can we escape from the torture of the visible, from the fragmentation and separation in separate time-frames.

The mark of a stamp pervades the novel to the very name of its hero. Nostromo/Nostr' Uomo is the product of a contraction, of faulty information received due to the linguistic lack of finesse of Captain Mitchell's ear. The stamp is audible in the chatter of the patriot parrots who frequent the Casa Gould, is visible in the impassive equestrian statue of Don Carlos, a commander who sends to their doom, to a feast of stones, the prancing figures who pass beneath his pedestal.

We should not look for profundity or attempt to decipher the consciousness – or the subconscious – of the characters in *Nostromo*. If we are wise, we will respect Conrad's geography of surfaces – will not try to smooth-over jagged edges. The best place from which to view them, of course, is from the fault-line, where the phenomena of fragmentation and contraction, inevitable complements of the literary stamping operation, are most visible. Rather than accepting its rugged geography, the fault-line is the very place, of course, which the phenomenological and dialectical philosophers in their keenness to exhaust visible reality, to produce it, would prefer to bridge.

For Conrad is not interested in total, totalitarian truth or in the raw immediacy of things in the outcome/output of the scientific process, the result of which is constantly delayed in its own production, but prefers, rather, to stay on the fault-line of determinations where breaks, time-frames, plications of strata, and sedimentations occur:

> On the occasion when the fires under the first set of retorts in their shed had glowed far into the night she did not retire to rest on the rough cadre set up for her in the as yet bare frame-house till she had seen the first spongy lump of silver yielded to the hazards of

the world by the dark depths of the Gould concession; she had laid her unmercenary hands, with an eagerness that made them tremble, upon the first silver ingot turned out still warm from the mould; and by her imaginative estimate of its power she endowed that lump of metal with a justificative conception, as though it were not a mere fact, but something far-reaching and impalpable, like the true expression of an emotion or the emergence of a principle.

Don Pepe, extremely interested, too, looked over her shoulder with a smile that, making longitudinal folds on his face, caused it to resemble a leathern mask with a benignantly diabolic expression. (p. 107)

The image of Mrs Gould giving the mineral substance her spiritual *fiat*, placing a gold seal on a silver ingot, is not only the celebration of a bimetallic communion but also an occasion for Conrad to stress the relationship which inevitably links what is valuable and what is visible, figures and coins, in this Western world of ours.

10 The Power of Writing

Their ears are dull and their eyes are closed

(*Matthew*)

Is it possible that you haven't seen that in this book I am concerned with nothing but ideas, to the exclusion of everything else, with no arrière-pensée of any kind?
Letter from Joseph Conrad to Edward Garnett, 20 October 1911

POWER, WRITING, SACRIFICE

Let us begin with the title of *Under Western Eyes*. A moment's reflection is enough to make you realise how unusual it is. Because it bears the imprint of an eye, it usually does not attract much attention. In the list of titles selected by Conrad it is unique, however, as we shall see. The usual Conradian title includes a name which immediately puts the reader on familiar terms with the hero or heroine. Sometimes, a title like *Nostromo*/our man indicates a long-standing acquaintance with the main character. The bond of solidarity which exists between the narrative and its subject is thus extended to include the reader, who is admitted into the circle of initiates, into a circle which he may consider to be a kind of Victorian club or a land of magic, depending on whether or not he chooses to associate the narrator with the ordinary present tense or with a more prestigious past.

In *Lord Jim* Marlow's conception of 'one of us' sets up the legitimacy of reading in terms of a Baudelairian brotherhood: 'mon semblable, mon frère'. Conrad creates a more personal and more human relationship than for example the Balzacian one in which family names take precedence. Although in Balzac's titles the family name is sometimes qualified by an affectionate diminutive like 'Old Goriot', it cannot fail to inspire a certain sense of respect, like the republican galaxies in the welkin of the birth registry. With

Conrad's 'one of us',[1] administrative inflexibility seems to loosen up somewhat and the surface veneer seems to crack, with the result names, unconnected to anything in the crumbling empire, seem to exist by themselves – the title *Lord Jim* does not have the same cutting impact as do titles with patronymic surnames like *Tom Jones* or *Moll Flanders*. In Conrad's works, surnames tend to disappear except in secondary works like 'Gaspar Ruiz' and 'Amy Foster'. Yet, the main prerogative of heroes is never really abandoned. If the titles no longer bear the names of specific human beings, with official birth certificates, they have symbolic and allegorical connotations, as in 'Youth', *Victory, Chance* and *Suspense*. The secret agent himself retains his power of action behind the screen of his anonymity.

And then we come to the exception of *Under Western Eyes*. The location which it designates is less easily defined than a more precise geographical area described in *'Twixt Land and Sea* or *Within the Tides*. The echo of eye/I can also be the source of some confusion, for the passive agent can be turned into an active one, the one being observed into the person doing the observing. It is a title without a verb; the eye is deprived of action and confined to the limited function of being a mere object. It is a title without a subject, a title 'under' the dominion of a preposition. Except for the rather vague adjective 'Western', it is an anonymous title. There is no direct object, no verbal complement, which is all the more frustrating as eyesight is not usually conceived of without an object of some kind. We usually see something, but in this case there is nothing which meets the eye. What are we to make of the title – and the novel. Do both lie under the eyes of the West? We could try and solve the problem rapidly by matching the Western half, the Western eye, with its Eastern counterpart, its shadow, its secret sharer. For our part, we prefer to applaud the syntactic *tour de force* which leaves the title bare of agent and complement. What is remarkable is the very absence of marks. The wisest course to follow is to keep an eye on the ambiguous eye that never stops watching from across the page.

POWER, TORTURE, BODIES

In *Nostromo*, physical torture is only experienced by two characters, Dr Monygham and the Jewish merchant Hirsch. (It is ironic that Monygham becomes an eye-witness to the sufferings endured by

Hirsch.) Suffering pervades the entire novel, however, due to the fact that in the double exploitation of mines and men, truth, which is based on the extortion of secrets, is inevitably linked to the economic and financial operations. In *Under Western Eyes*, torture appears as a favourite means of obtaining power. Governments practise all different kinds of mental and physical torments, with the main victim being the hero Razumov. Few tragic heroes have had the fate of exposing to such a degree the sadistic mechanism of power. In his case fate is not only singular. It is not one fate which destroys his life as an assiduous student at the University of St Petersburg but a convergence of fates. Just as Geneva, a neutral city, offers him both shelter and punishment, Razumov's tragic world is also a neutral one where passivity leads to self-destruction. An orphan, a hostage of life from the outset, he is later crushed by the infernal mechanism of autocracy and revolution. Razumov ceases to belong to himself and becomes the victim of contradictory and conflicting allegiances. He feels a sense of duty towards his protectors and employers; he feigns loyalty to the revolutionaries; his love for Natalia Haldin, the sister of the man he betrayed, is mixed with remorse. It is a tragic tangle, a tragic triangle. Razumov reaches the point where he is unable to take affirmative action of any kind. Paradoxically, but also logically, his salvation or disappearance are not really what matter in the story. Razumov is not so much a scapegoat as a touchstone for all the forces which crush him. His defeat reveals their infernal power to destroy human beings. Now we understand why Razumov, like any self-respecting Conradian hero, has less of a sacrificial value and more of an informative one. (He is an informer, isn't he?) Passivity in Razumov's case is not to be interpreted, as in classical tragedy, in terms of confrontation with the law or in terms of an eventual renewal of the law. Both anarchy and autocracy reflect and echo each other across the screen of his neutrality. Thus, it is quite significant that Nikita Necator, the revolutionaries' executioner and Razumov's torturer, should turn out to be a double-agent, a revolutionary in the service of the autocratic regime. Just as Lord Jim eventually falls under the spell of his double in the Manichean kingdom of romance, so Razumov receives the death blow from another double-agent, his antagonist and accomplice.

We should refrain, however, from interpreting that complicity on purely psychological or on purely ethical grounds. Although the figure of Rousseau looms in the background of the novel, Conrad's interest does not lie solely in human nature or in its sadistic and masochistic components. For Conrad, neutrality and passiveness only have a tragic meaning in so far as they indicate the degree of dependency to which human beings are reduced by the misuse of power. More important than the conflicts of aggressors and victims – whose roles are often interchangeable, the victims becoming torturers and vice versa – is the raw material of tortures and mutilations; i.e. the body which is in endless supply. Take the case of Councillor Mikulin, executioner of Nicholas Haldin, whose fall from favour turns him into a non-person, into a civil corpse: 'It seems that the savage autocracy, no more than the civil democracy does not limit its diet exclusively to the bodies of its enemies. It devours its friends and servants as well.' That is why the punishment inflicted by Necator on Razumov, whose broken eardrums leave him defenceless against the town traffic, appears to be the most perfected in a series of tortures which we had only learned about indirectly, on hearsay, in a muffled way as it were. There was the assassination of Monsieur de P — by Haldin:' there was a body dressed in a peasant's sheep-skin coat; but the face was unrecognizable'; as well as the suffering endured by the revolutionary lithographer who was nursed by Tekla: 'There was a crushed spirit in that mangled body' (Razumov, too, will end his life in Tekla's care). Such spectacular cases should not, however, prevent us from recognising an even more subtle form of human mutilation. The bodies of some of the characters in the book have been neutralised and bear little resemblance to living men and women. There is the Russian café-owner, 'a sort of sexless and shivering scarecrow' or the caretaker of the place where Razumov lives in St Petersburg, 'she was a short, thick, shapeless woman with a large yellow face wrapped up everlastingly in a black woollen shawl'; or, again, Madame de S— the egeria of Peter Ivanovitch, 'who produced at first view a strong effect by the deathlike immobility of an obviously painted face', and who is later compared to a galvanized corpse out of some Hoffman's Tale'. Still more significant is the reduction of parts of bodies to the state of objects. (No psychoanalytic or obsessive reference is intended.) The privileged parts of the body singled out for this kind of attention in *Under Western Eyes* are the eyes and the hands. At times, they seem to be endowed with a sort of autonomous, surrealistic power – like the hand of Razumov's protector: 'on getting out on the pavement Razumov saw an ungloved hand extended to him through the lowered window of the brougham. It detained its own in his grasp for a moment.' The goggle eyes of General T—have a magnetic power which Razumov's wax-like conscience is quick to retain: 'Have you ever reflected on the power of goggle eyes and grey whiskers? . . . It has happened to me once to be talking to a man whose face was affected by physical facts of that kind.' The significance of the body is a problem which Conrad confronts in all his works, but *Under Western Eyes* is perhaps the only one in which it is defined in philosophical terms. Seen in this light, Razumov's passiveness is not only a personal characteristic, but the symbol of a certain Cartesian '*epoche*', in which the very sense of the body itself has been lost. Razumov seems to be suffering from a personal schism in which the faculties of feeling and reasoning are disassociated.

This division leads him to seek the comfort of sense impressions

> the sense of life's continuity depended on trifling bodily impressions. The trivialities of daily existence were an armour for the soul. And this thought reinforced the inward quietness of Razumov as he began to climb the stairs familiar to his feet in the dark, with his hand on the clammy banister. The exceptional could not prevail against the material contacts which make one day resemble another. Tomorrow would be like yesterday. (pp. 53–4)

or to seek refuge in the rational logic of geometric reasoning which permits him to dispense with troublesome thoughts and ethical considerations: 'Is he laughing at me? Razumov asked himself, going on with his aimless drawing of triangles and squares.' Many other characters in the novel experience a similar phenomenon. In the case of Peter Ivanovitch, the anarchist who escaped from Tsarist prisons in Siberia, it takes the form of a conflict between nature and culture: 'the wild beast was making its way instinctively eastward to the Pacific Coast and the civilized humanitarian in fearful anxious dependence watched the proceedings with awe. Natalia Haldin has experienced similar sensations but manages to rise above them by creating a personal philosophy which takes into consideration all that is mysterious in human experience: ' "Everything is inconceivable", she said. "The whole world is inconceivable to the strict logic of ideas. And yet the world exists to our senses and we exist in it. There must be a necessity superior to our conceptions." '

In this novel, as in *Nostromo*, Conrad's major interest lies in flaws and faults, not in mending, in healing or ethical solutions. What we call a solution is really only a choice which produces further divisions and further mutilations. The Swiss downpour which ushers in Razumov's confession is much more than a mere aesthetic solvent: 'Razumov walked straight home on the wet glistening pavement. A heavy shower passed over him; distant lightning playing faintly against the front of the dumb houses with the shuttered shops all along the Rue de Carouge.' The compromise worked out between the unruffled lake waters of Razumov's reverie and the torrential storm of his confession are a tribute to the diplomatic influence of the Swiss capital, but even this cure of neutrality cannot miraculously restore the body to its health, and reverse this process of alienation for the Western neurosis is too deeply rooted:

> At that moment Razumov beheld his own brain suffering on the rack – a long pale figure, drawn asunder horizontally with terrific force in the darkness of a vault whose face he failed to see. It was as though he had dreamed for an infinitesimal fraction of time of some dark print of the Inquisition. (p. 88)

In other words, in alien words, what could Voltaire's Switzerland (or Cabaret) do against the swinging pendulum of 1911? Do not reason and inquisition come from the same pit? Pit/pendulum (Geneva, Boulevard des Nouveaux Philosophes 1978)?

NARRATION, VOYEURISM, CENSORSHIP

Geneva, the city that Scott Fitzgerald felt was at the centre of the Western Psychosis,[2] witnessed the arrival in 1907 of Joseph Conrad, who had come seeking a cure for a mental breakdown caused by the tension involved in writing *The Secret Agent*. His sojourn in Geneva led him to write *Under Western Eyes*. In 1922, T. S. Eliot left London for Margate and Lausanne hoping to restore a fragmented personality and to forget the desolation of 'The Waste Land'. Students of literary history are well aware that Ezra Pound advised Eliot not to use a phrase from Conrad's 'Heart of Darkness' as the epigraph to *The Waste Land*. This literary footnote to history should not be dismissed as irrelevant, for it reveals to what extent Pound had failed to understand Conrad and how Eliot, on the other hand, had penetrated to the very heart of the matter.[3] *The Waste Land* has its beginning in the end of Conrad's Geneva: 'By the waters of Leman I sat down and wept'. Razumov's journey from Russia, 'inanimate, cold, inert, like a sullen and tragic mother hiding her face under a winding sheet', to Geneva's Lake Leman, 'fed by the icy cold waters of the Arve, (which) falling over a low dam swept towards us with a chilly draught of air across the great open space', follows the itinerary of *The Waste Land* – though in the opposite direction – towards a protracted, painstaking renewal:

> In the very air through which she moved there was but little warmth; and the sky, the sky of a land without horizons, swept and washed clean by the April showers, extended a cold cruel blue without elevation, narrowed suddenly by the ugly dark wall of the Jura where, here and there, lingered yet a few miserable trails and patches of snow. (pp. 141–2)

Geneva is the land of a cruel spring where the promise of a renewed alliance with the forces of life can only be fulfilled through suffering and sacrifice, a land where eardrums will be burst, a prophetic punishment which is but the muffled echo of heavier, impending explosions. Although Eliot's *The Waste Land* lies under torrid skies, he uses a similar *geste* of seasons and a mythical spring of rebirth:

> April is the cruellest month, breeding
> Lilacs out of the dead land, mixing
> Memory and desire, stirring
> Dull roots with spring rain . . .

Joseph Conrad and T. S. Eliot echo each other across the Great Divide of the First World War, blending memory and prophecy. The anonymous voice from *The Waste Land*, 'I read much of the night and go south in the Winter', brings back memories of Tekla's pathetic complaint, 'Even when we move to the South of France there are bitterly cold days, especially when you have to sit still for six hours at a stretch. The walls of these villas are so flimsy.'

Under Western Eyes is probably the most subtle and the most complicated of Conrad's works; its symbolism has more than one register of meaning, and the imaginative process cannot be disassociated from the manner of presenting the narrative. A reported narrative, like many others in Conrad's works, it is told in a hesitating, halting voice by the Teacher of Languages whose sole presence lends an air of ambiguity to the intrigue. More far-sighted and sharp-minded than the Marlows of 'Heart of Darkness' and *Lord Jim*, he takes the story in hand right from the beginning, without waiting for anyone to designate him as the best-qualified person for the task. He begins his narrative with a self-portrait in which he describes himself as an extremely negative person whose principal characteristics are unassertiveness and lack of imagination. Curiously enough, even these negative qualities are obscured by the haste and pompousness with which he makes these modest claims. Moreover, his self-portrait does not include any biographical details; it is only in conversation with Razumov that he gives a full account of his origins:

> While waiting to be served, I mentioned that, born of parents settled in St. Petersburg, I had acquired the language as a child. The town I did not remember, having left it for good as a boy of nine, but in later years I had renewed my acquaintance with the language. . . . 'But you are an Englishman—a teacher of literature.' 'Quite true. More than twenty years. And I have been assisting Miss Haldin with her English studies.' (pp. 187–8)

Is the Teacher of Languages English, Russian or Jewish? He seems to be all of them, both at once and successively. He is an uprooted person, doomed to live in exile and to suffer from the amnesia of languages. He lives in a no-man's-land, in the middle, neutral ground that separates peoples and nations. His voice resembles closely the blank, colourless voice which is heard from the beginning to the end of *The Waste Land*. A spectator at life's feast, he suffers from a tragic form of paralysis that is much like Razumov's. He is a witness whose function is simply to record the events which unfold before his eyes. He has no pretension, as did the earlier Marlows, that he has any power to influence the protagonist of the story. The Teacher of Languages manages to overcome a certain amount of his timidity only when he abandons the story told in Razumov's diaries to give his own version of what actually happened. Even then, when the action takes place in Geneva, his home ground, and he is as close as he can be to the events, the sense of his own exclusion strikes him more acutely than ever: 'I felt profoundly my European remoteness and said nothing but I made up my mind to play my part of helpless spectator to the end.' The Teacher of Languages is subject to a fateful passivity which amounts to a form of mutilation that is all the more subtle for being dressed up in psychological terms, and excuses itself on the pretext of being neutral and objective. The Teacher of Languages seems to have perfected his negative virtues in a society where censorship and repression are rampant:

> To begin with I wish to disclaim the possession of those high gifts of imagination and expression which would have enabled my pen to create for the reader the personality of the man who called himself after the Russian custom Cyril, son of Isidor Kyrilo Sidorovitch Razumov. If I have ever had these gifts in any sort of living form, they have been smothered out of existence a long time ago under a wilderness of words. (p. 3)

Self-denegation is a favourite rhetorical mode with the narrator who seems to derive pleasure from his position as an outsider – his shelter of a hundred indecisions. It is relatively easy to catch him in the act of contradicting himself since he often lets himself be carried away by the very gift of imagination which he claims to lack. In spite of all his 'objective' principles, he imagines a number of scenes when he is unable to see the characters involved: 'I could imagine the motionless dumb figure of the mother in her chair, there behind the door, near which the daughter was talking to me.' Admittedly, his double status of insider and outsider is due to his neutrality, to an unexplained repression of sexual desire which comes to the surface from time to time in the form of a certain remorse. Natalia Haldin has roused an old spring fever in the frost-bound body crushed under the weight of words and language. Torn between the repression and the assertion of these feelings, he experiences both envy and regret in the astonishing scene in which Razumov, like Flaubert's Mathô, takes away Natalia/Salammbô's *zaimph*, or veil:

> At his feet the veil dropped by Miss Haldin looked intensely black in the white crudity of the light. He was gazing at it spellbound. Next moment, stooping with incredible, savage swiftness, he snatched it up and pressed it to his face with both hands. Something, extreme astonishment perhaps, dimmed my eyes, so that he seemed to vanish before he moved. The slamming of the outer door restored my sight and I went on contemplating the empty chair in the empty anteroom. The meaning of what I had

seen reached my mind with a staggering shock. I seized Natalia
Haldin by the shoulder. 'That miserable wretch has carried off
your veil,' I cried in the scared, deadened voice of an awful
discovery. (pp. 355–6)

Having demurely, virginally, stayed in the anteroom throughout
the scene, the narrator/translator is excluded and included, un-
decisive and undecided, on the threshold of hymen. A Tiresias
whose sight is dimmed, who lacks the lucidity of the tragic mantis of
The Waste Land, the Teacher of Languages has the role of a *voyeur*
during the symbolic rape of the veil: 'To Carthage then I came'.
Only the slamming of the outer door restores his sight and brings
him to his senses once more. His indecisiveness is the exact Western
counterpart of the Eastern passiveness instilled in Razumov by
many years spent under autocratic rule. It would be sheer blindness
on our part not to see that, far from being innocent in its criticism of
the evils of Russian tyranny, whether aristocratic or revolutionary,
the brand of liberal neutrality of which he is so proud exposes him in
turn to the criticism and censure of Natalia Haldin about the
dangers of democracy: 'There are nations that have made their
bargain with fate. You belong to a people which has made a bargain
with fate and would not like to be rude to it.' Taken out of the
Russian context, this statement may seem to have pretentious
overtones, but seen in the light of Miss Haldin's personal experience, it is a perceptive comment on the devaluation of heroism
in Western society, where neutrality is often synonymous with
mediocrity. We should not speak of duality here but imagine a
three-way relationship in which European neutrality is blind to the
complicity of East and West. Is it possible to consider that England
is present in the democratic desert of Switzerland? England is
present in its envoy the Teacher of Languages, of course. It could
also be said that the public walk of the Bastions, where so many
meetings and interviews take place, is a reminiscence of England
(do not forget that public walks and public gardens are an
institution of Protestant civilisations). England is vicariously present in the representative democratic couple (Parson Wiss's Swiss
Robinsons)[4] who are seen drifting on their tiny democratic facsimile
of a raft in a public park:

There was a quantity of tables and chairs displayed between the
restaurant chalet and the bandstand, a whole raft of painted deals

spread out under the trees. In the very middle of it I observed a solitary Swiss couple whose fate was made secure from the cradle to the grave by the perfected mechanism of democratic institutions in a republic that could almost be held in the palm of one's hand. (p. 175)

The seaworthiness – or lakeworthiness – of their secure craft is indeed based on deal(s), some of which should attract the attention of readers who believe that Conrad's portrayal of truth is to be found on the surface and encourage them to give the matter at least a second thought. For if, confronted as he is, by the blind faith of the revolutionaries in the power of revolutions, the narrator is entitled to maintain a certain sceptical reserve, isn't the refusal of the revolutionaries to imitate the parliaments of Western democracies, to create artificial conflicts, as legitimate?

We Russians shall find some better form of national freedom than an artificial conflict of parties which is wrong because it is a conflict and contemptible because it is artificial. It is left for us Russians to discover a better way. (p. 106)

Yet if Natalia Haldin overlooks the possibility, the third possibility, that a hitherto unknown type of autocracy might come to power in Russia, Conrad is not blind to that eventuality and suggests it in the geometry of this writing: 'Is he laughing at me? Razumov asked himself, going on with his aimless drawing of triangles and squares.' How innocent, how neutral can writing be?

WRITING, VIOLENCE, SUFFERING

Write. Must write! He! Write. A sudden light flashed upon him. To write was the very thing he had made up his mind to do that day. (p. 288)

On the edge of Lake Geneva whose clear waters hold a dangerous fascination for Razumov –,a stone on the bottom seems to indicate what the fates hold in store for him –the arrival of the anarchist Julius Laspara, who looks like a gnome or a genie just recently let out of a bottle, sets the stage for a strange encounter. Julius Laspara, 'Polyglot, of unknown parentage, of indefinite nationality, with a

pedantic and ferocious temperament and an amazingly inflam-
matory capacity for invective, clamouring for revolutionary justice,
editor of the *Living Word*, urges Razumov to write something:
'Write in Russian. We'll have it translated . . . There can be no
difficulty. Why, without seeking further, there is Miss
Haldin . . . Only write. You know you must. And so good-bye for
the present.' Under the spell of that dreamlike encounter,
Razumov continues his solitary walk as far as Jean-Jacques
Rousseau's island, which curiously enough, has the form of an elbow
bent at an angle and prolonged by a short forearm:

> This [bridge] much narrower than the other and instead of being
> straight, made a sort of elbow or angle. At the point of that angle a
> short arm joined it to a hexagonal islet with a soil of gravel and its
> shores faced with dressed stone, a perfection of puerile neatness.
> (p. 290)

The image is a striking one. It is an almost surrealistic ankylosis
(Switzerland is where automats originated), a contraction of
historical and psychological aspects of the writer's art. Rousseau's
Confessions are often referred to when dealing with Razumov's
experience, but they are really less relevant than the *Social Contract*.
Razumov's promenade, from the point where he sees the stone on
the bottom of the lake to the statutory and statuary island, takes him
into the democracy of writing, a shagreen republic, 'a republic that
could almost be held in the palm of one's hand' so that Julius
Laspara's order to write something, which preceded his retreat to
the island, does not mark the hero's conversion to a new way of life
so much as it points out the main obsession of the book, writing.
Under Western Eyes is Conrad's most accurate and subtle analysis of
the bond linking the writer to his art. The intrigue is only a pretext
and cannot be analysed according to traditional literary canons.

Under Western Eyes is a tragedy, of course, a tragedy which begins
with a mistake and ends with a punishment in accordance with
established tradition. Yet, the main concern of the novel is
nevertheless with writing, and its power to distort as well as depict
reality. Writing. Why, everybody is writing something in *Under
Western Eyes* – under the supervision of a master writer, the Teacher
of Languages and Literature who acts as the co-ordinator of the
various stories. Councillor Mikulin sits in his private office in the
midst of a 'lot of scribbling' and welcomes Razumov 'with a

penholder in his hand'. In its telegraphic form, writing spells death for Haldin, who refused to write a confession although he was offered 'some sheets of grey foolscap'. With Peter Ivanovitch, who escaped from prisons like Bakunin and Kropotkin, writing can only take the epic form. Although the Teacher of Languages uses a mocking tone to describe the literary efforts of Peter Ivanovitch, his imagination is none the less roused to a nightmarish pitch: 'this big pinkish poll evoked for me the vision of a wild head with matted locks peering through parted bushes . . . It was an involuntary tribute to the vigours of his writing.' Razumov indulges in the daily exercise of diary-keeping, but how do we go about describing the role played by Razumov's legatee, the Teacher of Languages, in making use of his sources? Does he tamper with them, for instance? The problem of truth and lying is not Conrad's chief concern. Although constant use is made of such rhetorical devices as denegation and understatement in the quiet teacher's case, they are only used to divert the reader's attention. Writing is an obsession that goes beyond the mere multiplication of narrators and narratives, however, and is also presented through the iterative rhythm of symbols and images. The Teacher of Languages, a man of paper, is compulsively on the alert at the slightest rustling noise and feels compelled to investigate even what is incomprehensible to him: 'The letter rustled slightly in her hand. I glanced down at the flimsy blackened page whose very handwriting seemed cabalistic, incomprehensible to the experience of Western Europe.' He is a man of paper who seeks shelter in libraries, in the anterooms of action. He is a man of paper who is wary of being present, in the flesh, among his equals and who prefers whenever possible to send a letter in place of his person:

> The middle-aged servant woman led me into the drawing room where there was a duster on a chair and a broom leaning against the centre table. The motes danced in the sunshine. I regretted I had not written a letter instead of coming myself, and was thankful for the brightness of the day. (p. 111)

A man of paper from beginning to end, he refers incessantly to what constitutes his own being. According to him, the desert-like immensity of Russia is a white page waiting for the inscription of historical events: 'like a monstrous blank page awaiting the record of an inconceivable history'. The face of Monsieur de P— Haldin's

victim, 'with a face of crumpled parchment', and the eyes the colour
of ink of Sophia Antonovna – 'the very spirit of restless revolution
embodied in that woman with her white hair and black eyebrows,
like slightly sinuous lines of Indian ink, drawn together by the
perpendicular folds of a thoughtful frown' – are also visualised in
terms of the writer's craft. The icy surface of Lake Geneva is a
manuscript soon to be disturbed by the violent Arve of
confession: 'the expanding space of water to the right with jutting
promontories of no particular character had the uninspiring,
glittering quality of a very fresh oleograph.'

Conrad's achievement here is to make writing perceptible and
inperceptible at the same time. His interest in writing is likely to pass
unnoticed by the majority of readers, even today, as they de-
sperately try to follow the confusing directions given in the title.
What can the West possibly be looking for if not the East, is how
they interpret that enigmatic phrase. Now, if the text is to be
properly understood, a reading revolution will have to take place.
In speaking of this text, we can truthfully say that 'The letter
killeth', for the complicity of author and killers is quite evident.
There is Nikita Necator, the professional killer who prints the seal of
his initials on his victims, the writer of death and crime who is almost
completely illiterate, 'Nikita nicknamed Necator with a sinister
aptness of alliteration'. There are other killers who also refuse to sign
their full names and prefer to hide their criminal potential behind
one or two initials. These anonymous characters who all have good
reasons for wishing to remain anonymous are Prince K—,
Razumov's protector, General T—, Head of the Police, and
Monsieur de P— , the President of the Repressive Commission.
Another, even more bloodthirsty character, who calls for the
extermination of her enemies is Madame de S— , the egeria of the
anarchists in Geneva:

> 'As to extirpating', she croaked at the attentive Razumov, 'there
> is only one class in Russia which must be extirpated. Only one.
> And that class consists of one family. You understand me? That
> one family must be extirpated.'

In *Under Western Eyes*, Conrad makes an exhaustive investigation of
the relationship between writing, power, and truth. His mistrust of
heroism, and of truth through suffering, of the Gospel truth (is it
possible to accept the fact that the spirit should be conquered

through the lethal power of the letter?), is fundamental. In the heroic scheme of things, the truth becomes the truth according to those who lord it over their servants – who sacrifice themselves in order that the truth might be revealed. Peter Ivanovitch has his secretary Tekla writhe on the rack of her desk in the name of anarchist principles:

> But you have not been behind the scenes. Wait till you have to sit at a table for a half-day with a pen in your hand. . . .
>
> After taking down Peter Ivanovitch from dictation for two years, it is difficult for me to be anything. First of all, you have to sit perfectly motionless. The slightest movements you make puts to flight the ideas of Peter Ivanovitch. You hardly dare to breathe. . . . The trying part of it was to have the secret of the composition laid bare before her: to see the great author of the revolutionary gospels grope for words as if he were in the dark as to what he meant to say. (pp. 146–8)

Miserable writing! Miserable printing, responsible for the torturing power of letters to set free the imagination.

For Joseph Conrad, no argument, no theory about the sacredness of art can hide the fact that the imagination is freed only after an act of deliberate sacrifice. This sacrifice resembles and reproduces itself. Thus Tekla, chained by her master Ivanovitch to her desk and forced to listen to him all day long, manages somehow to force Natalia Haldin to listen to the narrative of her own sufferings, which revolve, ironically enough, around the story of a lithographer! The Victorian form of slavery which has Tekla serve both as cook and secretary seems to favour the development of an anarchist Carrollian strain in her imagination. Ironically, only the relentless turning of the screws and the eternal grinding of the presses can produce a *geste* of the spirit, whether it be fantastic or epic.

Conrad mistrusts both the Christian and the revolutionary canons, but he is no admirer of the other face of the Western coin which is stamped with the commerical values of calculation and trade. The absence of death in the monetary scheme of things is only an illusion; death does not strike directly but indirectly, with the result that no one dare accept responsibility for what society prefers to put in the anonymous hands of collective management. A distinguished advocate of this linguistic and monetary system, the Teacher of Languages, like the messengers of classical tragedy, is a harbinger of death. Unlike them, he is an unwitting, unconscious informer, surprised at the lethal consequences of his acts, who does not experience feelings of guilt when things go awry. Standard-bearing in his case means carrying the *Standard* around in his pocket. The respectable paper of the man of paper is the anonymous tool of chance disclosures:

> I pulled the paper out of my pocket. I did not imagine that a number of the Standard could have the effect of Medusa's head . . . I confess that my real sympathy had no standpoint. The reader for whom this story is written will understand what I mean. It was, if I may say so, the want of experience. Death is a remorseless spoliator. The anguish of irreparable loss is familiar to us all. There is no life so lovely as to be safe against that experience. But the grief I had brought to these two ladies had gruesome associations. It had associations of bombs and gallows – a lurid Russian colouring which made the complexion of my sympathy uncertain. (p. 111)

This confession is a model of hypocrisy – and naïveté. He passes himself off as a simple mediator – a media man – who, on the pretext of being objective, systematically refuses all contact with the body of truth. In his voyeuristic philosophy imagination is to exist only in others and to be repressed in oneself, becoming in the process a kind of exotic commodity subject to sociological or anthropological analysis. We realise of course that behind the surface irony directed against himself – 'dense Westerner' and the like, which in the end makes the revolutionaries look all the more foolish – lies a basic, tragic inability to disentangle himself from his role of exchanging, circulating and passing on pieces of information: pieces of truth. Jean-Jacques Rousseau made a similar criticism of Western writing. In His 'L'Essai sur l'Origine des Langues', analysed by Jacques Derrida in *De la Grammatologie*,[5] Rousseau thinks of writing as an activity closely linked to the degradation of the primitive social bond, with writing progressively replacing the immediacy and spontaneity of words, just as the values of Communal life were progressively replaced by exchange, commerce and the delegation of authority in the modern social order. Natalia Haldin, too, has a similar outlook, as we see in her criticism of the relationship which unites the press, the financial circles and the ruling factions in Western society. Conrad gives the irony one final twist by underlining the contracting power of writing, so deplorable in Rousseau's eyes, on, of all places, the tiny hand-shaped island named for Rousseau himself.

Under Western Eyes. Eyes without body, without any body. Because the respective and complementary truths which Western and Eastern societies have discovered dispense with the body which is offered to the holocaust of the law. Unless it be pawned against the currency of indifference in the inexhaustible circulation of names. Either heroes or bank clerks. Either Hamlets or Prufrocks.

Words, words, words (*Hamlet*)

Words, as is well known, are the great foes of reality. I have been for many years a teacher of languages. It is an occupation which at length becomes fatal to whatever share of imagination, observation and insight an ordinary person may be heir to. To a teacher of languages, there comes a time when the world is but a place of many words and man appears a mere talking animal not much more wonderful than a parrot. . . . But I must apologise for this digression. (*Under Western Eyes*, pp. 3–4)

11 Conclusion

Absent from the scene of history for fourteen hours, during which the city of Sulaco is attacked by rebels, Nostromo, the henchman of Western capitalism, the latest copy of man fresh from the mould of Creation, pulls himself to his feet in the fulness of his mythic sovereignty:

> Nostromo woke up from a fourteen hours' sleep, and arose full length from his lair in the long grass. He stood knee deep amongst the whispering undulations of the green blades with the lost air of a man just born into the world. Handsome, robust and supple, he threw back his head, flung his arms open, and stretched himself with a slow twist of the waist and a leisurely growling yawn of white teeth, as natural and free from evil in the moment of waking as a magnificent and unconscious wild beast. Then, in the suddenly steadied glance fixed upon nothing, from under a thoughtful frown appeared the man. (*Nostromo*, pp. 411–12)

There is a reference to the Creation, of course, but this passage also brings to mind aspects of a 'Second Coming' and looks back to some of the greatest heroes of the century. In Nostromo's lineage, we could include Victor Hugo's Gilliat, even though Nostromo's adventures do not include death by drowning, as well as Fenimore Cooper's Leatherstocking, who preceded him to the grassy borders of the setting sun. Yet, in spite of these heroic ancestors, several ill-omens warn us of what will befall Nostromo. First of all, his awakening takes place at nightfall, a time that is more propitious for the reckoning up of accounts than for starting anew. Secondly, the vulture 'rey zamuro' which hovered over his slumber is the symbol of both death and the predatory instincts. Curiously enough, the visions of Promethean suffering and revolt implied by the presence of the vulture are apparently neutralised by the arrival of a bird of the night, an owl flying from the opposite direction in the dusk.

Thus, what we will call 'Nostromo's 'Second Coming' is an ironic event or advent, as you will. Conrad's use of several myths is enough to shatter the legitimacy and dignity of this man who would be a hero. Here begins the reign of the servants who, to borrow, the expression of Hegel, were formerly employed in taking off their masters' boots. In Nostromo's awakening there is a revolt against slavery, both the functional and the instrumental kinds: 'There is no mistake. They keep us and encourage us as if we were dogs born to fight and hunt for them.' Along with the 'revulsion of subjectiveness', Nostromo's senses are also roused and his body is resurrected. It is with the Mediterranean resilience of a Scapin that Nostromo wakes up on the beach of Sulaco – a beautiful animal recruited from the school of Darwin. Yet the call for subversion, the signal which announces the dawn of a new century and ushers in the epoch of the absurd, bears within itself its own limits. In the first place, the emancipation of servants does not necessarily free them from imitating their former masters: the second form of servility can be even more tragic than the first. Witness the case of the eleventh hour marxist confessor who is exposed, like one of his own photographs, in all his ape-like negativity:

> There was no one with the wounded man but the pale photographer, small, frail, bloodthirsty, the hater of capitalists, perched on a high stool near the head of the bed with his knees up and his chin in his hands. 'Do not forget that we want money for our work. The rich must be fought with their own weapons.' Nostromo made no answer. The other did not insist, remaining huddled up on the stool, shock-headed, wild-hairy, like a hunchbacked monkey. (p. 562)

Then the emancipation results in a false semblant of sovereignty, in a powerless state that is more debilitating than was the former bondage. Nostromo wakes up physically intact, with his body fully restored, but his advent takes place under the shadow of death: 'The confused and intimate impressions of universal dissolution which beset a subjective nature at any strong check to its ruling passions had a bitterness approaching that of death itself.' The fragmentation of Nostromo's personality, which resembles the metal-refining process itself, eventually separates his destiny from that of the mine. The account of Nostromo's fate underlines Conrad's belief that Reason cannot fully render human experience. In his work, mining values and human ones are not equated by means of some ingenious rational trick. The validity of the rational system and Reason as a diabolic power are both examined thoroughly. In other words, how can truth, like a mythical body continually dismembered and remembered, like Dionysus and Apollo, be born out of the conjunction of restlessness and rest:

> Thus the truth is like the bacchic delirium in which all the limbs are drunk; and since that delirium resolves in itself immediately each moment that tends to get separated from the whole – such delirium has also the transparency and simplicity of a rest.[1]

Does not such a philosophy which interprets truth as a kind of accumulation or as a kind of hoarding of reality – 'The truth is not like newly coined currency which is ready to be spent and collected'[2] – lead to confusion between bodies and signs, to a case of mistaken identities? Does it not integrate all too lightheartedly into the circuit of the production and the exchange of signs the notion of death, a never-ending organic expense?

> truth should not be considered as some dead theory. It manifests itself in the action of being born and of dying. It is not born and does not die, but the cyclic movement inherent in it makes it real for us and assures the very life of truth.[3]

If the absurdity of life is never depicted to its full extent in Conrad's work but is pathetically repressed and contained within the bounds of social adventure, it may be because, for Conrad, involving oneself in something either for the sake of Reason or for the sake of rebellion is a ludicrous gesture. Only death is really worth questioning and Conrad questions it from *its* point of view – which is fundamentally ironic. To accuse Conrad of exoticism on the pretext that his is an impossible goal is to forget that this is precisely the nature of the diabolic challenge of Romanticism.

When a writer no longer believes in the myth of heroism, when the fictional universe which was created around the intercessory power of an exemplary being begins to disintegrate, what then becomes the subject of writing? If, as Razumov says to Sophia Antonovna, irony, which is absolute negation,[4] is disliked by women, children and revolutionaries, what new mediator, what other victim, will take upon himself the excess of irony which our naïve modern world is so ill-equipped to bear? Whatever else may be said for him, a retarded child like Stevie does not have the power of healing or even the power of acting as an antidote against the dissolving action of the secret ferments, of the secret agents, at work in the Western world. Conrad's conception of irony, which flatly contradicts Hegel's idea of basic inequality,[5] is based on resemblances, on the lucid belief that many diverse phenomena are not really so different after all. Official power and anarchy in Victorian London, or in Tsarist Russia, are very much alike; revolutionary anarchism and the mediocrity of Western mercantilism co-exist in Geneva to such an extent that it is often difficult to distinguish one from the other. That is why Conrad abandons heroes as well as heroism, which he foresees taking, in centuries to come, a collective and anonymous form. Instead he exploits a reserve of untapped energy, a lucid acceptance of the power of negation, which until then had not been employed in the English novel. *Under Western Eyes* is a powerful testimony to one of the major concerns in Conrad's work – the act of writing itself – for this act, in its use of negative force, implies duplicity.

How does Conrad manage to escape from the dialectics of non-creation when, rejecting heroism as being totally inappropriate, he finds himself obliged to look for a means of imitating it in a negative mode? What he tries to put aside in portraying a whole international gallery of doubles like Razumov, Peter Ivanovitch, Julius Laspara and the Teacher of Languages, who reflect one another as well as their author, is his own ironic superiority. For Conrad, the act of duplicity takes the form of an unhappy human consciousness which ruptures and divisions have forced into the lonely positions of being an eternal onlooker: 'fated to be a spectator'. If we bear this in mind we realise that the distance which separates Razumov from the Teacher of Languages – in spite of the latter's insistence that he is cut off from the Eastern World – is a minimal one, an artificial one which dissimulates large areas of common ground. The eye, the third eye, the evil eye . . . perhaps no other writer, in his practice of writing, has come so close to the logic of his own writing. Perhaps no other writer has so attentively watched himself watching. Does that mean that for Conrad the subject of writing – 'a perfection of duplicity', to quote Razumov – is the devil himself? After all, the devil in his different metamorphoses is really the only being who remains equal to himself in all his guises, whether they be social, national, cultural or political. Like the devil, Conrad's subjects take on many different forms: if a beastly countenance is given to

Ziemanitch, the Russian peasant, a familiar and domestic one to Razumov, a humanistic and abstract one to the Teacher of Languages, a certain diabolic presence continually twists the terms of the contract, of the pact with the reader. In this 'oculists's interview', an occult figure whets the reader's curiosity and reveals to him how myopic his vision is.

To see, to make people see – visibility is *the* Western obsession in Conrad's eyes. In making it the aesthetic goal of his art, he renders its obsessive nature all the more obvious. Conrad's extreme lucidity permits him to see that there is a monstrous side to the act of writing. He was able to make this quite clear in a fascinating letter to Edward Garnett:

> The more I write the less substance do I *see* in my work. *The scales are falling off my eyes*. It is tolerably awful. And I *face* it, I *face* it but the fright is growing on me. My fortitude is shaken by *the view of the monster*. It does not move; its *eyes* are baleful; it is as still as death itself – and it will devour me. Its *stare* has eaten into my soul already deep, deep – I am alone with it in a chasm with perpendicular sides of black basalt – Never were sides so perpendicular and smooth, and high. Above, your anxious head against a bit of sky *peers down* – in vain – in vain. There's no rope long enough for that rescue [*my italics*].[6]

In his works, the irony corresponds to the most exaggerated form of the 'monstrous' process – when a pair of watching eyes has no other object than itself. (In *Under Western Eyes*, the staring eyes of General T — keep goggling and leave an indelible imprint on Razumov.) Yet, it would be yielding to a classic Western temptation to try and exorcise that evil eye by circumscribing it within the inevitable Oedipian triangle, to consider as simply the effect of some painful castration. Conrad's branch of anarchism is far too radical to take the form of a simple rebellion against parental authority. Although Jim, like Heyst, may sometimes seem unable to assert his own personality because of his prolonged adolescence, the actual folly of writing has little to do with that human, far too human, trinity whose foundations can be so easily demolished by irony. More difficult to identify is the hidden Secret Agent who tries to undo the author's duplicity, the voyeur who is for ever doomed to remain in the dark about himself, or will only know himself retrospectively.

It is important to recognise the generative power of absolute negativity in Conrad's writing. Harnessed by Hegel to produce truth, negativity – a powerful agent of death constantly surpassing its own expectations – never ceases, in its multiple manifestations, to remain identical to itself:

> Splitting and dividing is the work of our understanding. It is the most powerful activity that be, it is absolute power – Death, if this is the name we want to give that unreality, is the most awesome thing and to hold together what is dead is what requires the greatest amount of energy.[7]

Conrad's ironic power stems from his ability to make all the primitive anxiety concerning death his own and to ensure that this anxiety is ever present in his writing. In the novels, beginning with *Lord Jim* and up until *Under Western Eyes*, Conrad writes about the lack of heroes and heroism by exposing the frailty of the mediators who are doubles or figures of duplicity like Marlow/Kurtz, Marlow/Jim, and the Teacher of Languages/Razumov. Pointing to the lack of harmony between a force and its vectors, Conrad tries to show us that the Western viewpoint is haunted by a negative and deathlike presence which his irony has the role of revealing in all its excessive manifestations. The folly of searching for absolute truth, visible in the sovereign eye which gives *Nostromo* its basic unity, indicates that there are spheres where the diabolic and the celestial come together – God's and the Devil's acres. Conrad's supreme achievement is to have brought the notion of exhaustiveness – the goal of both science and the novel in the nineteenth century – to such a high pitch of intensity that, in spite of temporary retreats to the domestic hearths of contemporary absurdity, it is possible to discern the premises of a new logic and of a new method in his work – one which shuttles back and forth across the 'Shadow Line'.

Notes

1. *Tales of Unrest.*
2. I refer here to Bernard Noël's expression 'mort-mot' (death-word) which he uses in his preface to Roger-Gilbert Lecomte's essay 'Arthur Rimbaud' (Montpellier: Fata Morgana, 1972).
3. 'Voilà pourquoi je suis tellement un écrivain anglais se prêtant peu à la traduction. Un écrivain national comme Kipling par exemple se traduit facilement. Son intérêt est dans le sujet, l'intérêt de mon oeuvre est dans l'effet qu'elle produit' (letter to Henry Davray, 26 January 1908, in *Lettres Françaises de Joseph Conrad* edited by Georges Jean Aubry (Paris: Gallimard, 1930).
4. 'Mon point de vue, aussi bien sur terre que sur mer, est anglais mais il ne faut pas en conclure que je suis devenu anglais. Cela n'est pas. Le "homo duplex" a, dans mon cas, plus d'un sens. Vous me comprendrez. Je ne m'étends pas sur cette question' (letter to K. Waliszewski, 5 December 1903, in Aubry, op. cit.
5. 'M. Conrad juge d'une façon assez sévère le rôle que les races blanches de tous pays prétendent assumer vis à vis des races noires ou jaunes. Mais s'il montre un croiseur jetant une pluie de boulets sur quelques paillottes, où il est censé introduire les bienfaits de la civilisation, ce croiseur se trouve battre pavillon français, et l'on ne saurait dire qu'il y ait là du *fair play*' (K. Waliszewski 'Un cas de naturalisation littéraire', *La Revue* – Formerly *Revue des Revues* – no. 6, 15 December 1903.
6. 'Si je dis que le navire qui bombardait la côte était français c'est tout simplement parce que *c'était* un navire français. Je me rappelle son nom: le Seignelay. C'était pendant la guerre(!) du Dahomey. La réflexion qui suit s'appliquerait à un navire de toute autre nationalité, (Letter to K. Waliszewski, 16 December 1903, Aubry, op. cit.).
7. ' "Heart of Darkness" is experience, too; but it is experience pushed a little (and only very little) beyond the actual facts of the case for the perfectly legitimate, I believe, purpose of bringing it home to the minds and bosoms of the readers' ('Heart of Darkness', Author's Note, 1917).
8. See the French translation by Georges Jean-Aubry and André Ruyters. The pluperfect tense used by Conrad and 'imperfectly' rendered in French by the past present should be kept since it implies that, before the author himself did so, no one had accused Marlow of being anything but 'perfect'.
9. 'It lies on me to confess at last, and this is as good a place for it as another, that I have been all my life – all my two lives – the spoiled adopted child of Great Britain and even of the Empire; for it was Australia that gave me my first command' (Conrad's 'Author's Note' to 'Heart of Darkness', 1917).

10. 'Il parle de *ses compatriotes*. Moi j'écris *pour eux*. Donc lui peut très bien intéresser les étrangers – pour moi c'est bien plus difficile – peut-être impossible' (letter to Henry Davray, Aubry, op. cit.).

11. 'I write as I walk because I want to get somewhere and I write as straight as I can, just as I walk as straight as I can' (H. G. Wells, *Experiment in Autobiography*, London: Jonathan Cape, 1934).

12. In his preface to the account made by Jules Saintoyant, the man whom Brazza had selected to help him investigate the 'Affaire du Congo' in 1905, Charles André Julien writes: 'One cannot help evoking Conrad's story 'Heart of Darkness' about that philanthropist who went to the Belgian Congo in order to reclaim the natives and eventually turned into a slave-dealer before dying with these words "The horror! the horror!"' (Paris: L'Epi, 1960).

13. See *Under Western Eyes* and Chapter 10 in 'Analysis of the West'.

CHAPTER 2   AN INTOXICATING TALE

1. For centuries the route from Newcastle to London was the coal route and for nine years Captain Cook sailed it : until he came to prefer 'raw life' to 'cooked' life.

2. Arthur Rimbaud, 'Une Saison en Enfer'.

3. The title was suggested by Jacques Berque's *l'Orient Second* (Paris: Gallimard, 1970).

4. 'C'est finement vu et c'est exprimé avec finesse – presque a mots couverts . . . ', in C. T. Watts, Letters to Joseph Conrad's Cunninghame Graham, 7 January 1898 (Cambridge University Press, 1969).

CHAPTER 3   THE ENCLOSURE OF DEATH

1. This is a reference to the South Sea Bubble scandal of eighteenth-century fame, a financial scandal in which Walpole was the only one to float back to firm ground.

2. Thus the moon appears as a 'perfect disk' 'glowing ruddily' in Chapter 21, then appears again in a similar dramatic setting as an 'ascending spirit out of a grave; its sheen descended, cold and pale, like the ghost of dead sunlight' in Chapter 24, then becomes part of some abstract oriental landscape in Chapter 34: 'the bare contorted limb of some tree, growing on the slope, made a black crack right across its face'.

3. Every critic is indebted to the analysis of Northrop Frye in his *Anatomy of Criticism*, which tends, however, to neglect the technical aspect of Marlow's narration and the kind of dual relationship in which such narration involves the hero.

4. As is implicit in all structural analyses, whose merit is high indeed in so far as they have helped readers 'get their noses' out of the moral identifications critics used to be so fond of, but whose neutral position should now be abandoned. In the case of Jim, Marlow and Kurtz see for instance Wayne C. Booth's *Rhetoric of Fiction* (University of Chicago Press, 1961).

5. See the beginning of Chapter 21: 'There's many a heavenly body in the lot

crowding upon us of a night . . . '; or the reference made to 'the mysterious conjunctions of the planets' in Chapter 33, not to mention the countless apparitions of the moon throughout the novel. Cf. Note 2 above.

6. Chapter 36, in which the tale is as it were 'handed over', in which it is inherited like a legacy by the privileged listener, is shot through with elements of Baudelairian apocalypse, death striking its toll at a town clock. One might even go so far as to imagine, so slight is the distance separating Marlow from that 'correspondent', that it is Marlow himself who, coming back home from Patusan, finds that his own mail has caught up with him. But then that 'duplication' would have spelt the end of the book, whereas it is imperative that the tale should somewhere keep some open space, some issue outside itself.

7. In the Babel of *Lord Jim* the fragmentation of languages is an element of comedy (see the half-caste taking Jim to Patusan, the Patna captain, Stein himself). As to Jim, his return to the world of romance goes along with regression into the stereotyped language of light holiday literature which is part and parcel of that comedy while carrying overtones of the public school speech used by the Empire's 'old boys'. However, Jim's inarticulate stammering' ('He was not articulate', Chapter 22) is more or less pleonastic in relation to his own life, the stuff of which is ruptures and breaks. Marlow to Jim in Chapter 22: 'I told him that if he owed this chance to anyone especially, it was to an old Scot of whom he had never heard, who had died many years ago, of whom little was remembered besides a roaring voice.' Jim is someone that one cuts short in order to speak in his stead ('I cut him short. He was not articulate'), someone confined in space, in a reservation. The traders Marlow and Stein, nostalgic men, want to have Jim speak like a book while speaking themselves from the 'binding'. They reinvest, recycle actual deaths (here the old Scotsman's) into the ideal enclosure so that the myth of the quest may flourish and bloom. It is not until Kurtz's last journey that such articulateness will be exposed and the colonial book come to an end.

8. One of Marlow's friends who gives shelter to Jim following the latter's trial seems to hint at the hero's virgin-like nature, treating him as a 'young girl' for the purpose of a psychological portrait: 'Had he been a girl – my friend wrote – one could have said he was blooming – modestly – like a violet, not like some of these blatant tropical flowers' (Chapter 18). As to the last image of Jim remembered by Marlow (Chapter 35), it is one of immaculate whiteness in the stronghold of the night, an image similar to the one the narrator gave us at the opening.

CHAPTER 4   DEVIATIONS

1. As Marthe Robert says in *l'Ancien et le Nouveau* (Paris: Payot, 1967), 'La ruse est ici à demi avouée et s'il est vrai comme on le suppose parfois qu'ayant eu maille à partir avec l'Inquisition dés 1857, Cervantes a été excommunié, poursuivi, emprisonné par ses techniciens vigilants, on conçoit qu'il ait pris des détours prudents pour exprimer sa pensée.' This quotation to be completed by another, 'Le verbe, voilà donc la vraie religion de Don Quichotte'.

2. 'En sortant en effet Don Quichotte ne vise à rien moins qu'à redonner une norme au monde anarchique de son époque' (ibid.).

3. Jacques Le Goff has an exciting chapter on 'Structures Spatiales et Temporelles' in his *La Civilisation de l'Occident Médieval* (Paris: Arthaud, 1964).

4. In his *Jouvences sur Jules Verne* (Paris: Editions de Minuit, 1974) Michel Serres has written a stimulating book on travelling and desire. I am not certain whether I have not unconsciously quoted him here and there. 'Oui, la littérature vivait des terres inconnues, des rencontres possibles, de l'ubiquité interdite, de la suspension du désir: de ce qui résistait au décodage . . . Elle meurt de la fin des voyages et de la fin, en vue, de tout transport.'

5. See Pierre Gallais, in 'Perceval et l'Initiation' (Paris: Editions du Sirac, 1972) and more especially the chapter 'Du signifiant au signifié'.

6. More especially in Albert Pauphilet, *La Queste del S. Graal*, Les Classiques Français du Moyen-Age (Paris: Chamption, 1963).

7. Ibid.

8. *Perceval le Gallois ou le Conte du Graal*, (translated by Lucien Foulet (Paris: Nizet, 1900) 'Le Graal qui allait devant était de l'or le plus pur; des pierres précieuses y étaient serties, des plus riches et des plus variées qui soient en terre ou en mer; nulle gommes ne pourrait se comparer à celle du graal'.

9. 'La Quete du Graal' in Tzvetan Todorov, *Poètique de la Prose* (Paris: le Seuil, 1971).

CHAPTER 5   REVERSALS

1. 'La Quête du Graal' quoted by Tzvetan Todorov, *Poètique de la Prose* (Paris: Le Seuil, 1971).

2. Rudyard Kiplings 'The Roman Centurion's Song' in *A Choice of Kipling's Verse* edited by T. S. Eliot, (London: Faber and Faber, 1941).

3. Tim Jeal, *Livingstone* (London: Heinemann, 1973).

4. Marthe Robert, *Roman des Origines et origines du Roman* (Paris: Grasset, 1972).

5. Alan Moorehead, *The White Nile* (London: Hamish Hamilton, 1960).

6. Jules Saintoyant, 'L'Affaire du Congo'; see chapter 1, note 12.

7. W. S. Gilbert and Arthur Sullivan, *The Mikado*, 1885.

8. Isn't it a strange coincidence that one of the last adventurers of this age should have been called 'Papillon' (Mr Butterfly).

CHAPTER 6   SHORT-CUTS

1. That master brick-maker takes part in the building of the colonial Babel on top of which stands Kurtz. One may compare this image to the Biblical myth.

2. Joseph Conrad, 'Geography and Some Explorers' in *Last Essays*.

3. H. G. Wells, *Experiment in Autobiography* (London: Jonathan Cape, 1934, 1963).

4. One should think of Lewis Carroll's butcher turning to snark-hunting.

5. See Joseph Conrad's very interesting letter to Cunninghame Graham, dated 26 December 1903 in which Conrad assesses the Belgian colonisation in relation to Pizarro's adventure: Leopold is their Pizarro, Thys their Cortez and their 'lances' are recruited amongst the souteneurs, sous-offs, maquereaux, fruits-secs of all sorts on the pavements of Brussels and Antwerp. I send you two letters I had from a man called Casement premising that I knew him first in the Congo

just 12 years ago. Perhaps you've heard or seen in print his name. He's a protestant Irishman, pious too. But so was Pizarro. For the rest I can assure you that he is a limpid personality. There is a touch of the Conquistador in him too'.

6. See Edward Said, *Conrad's Struggle with Narrative* (Providence, Brown University Press, 1974).
7. See Frantz Fanon, *Peaux Noires, Masques Blancs* (Paris: Le Seuil, 1952).

CHAPTER 7   FULL CIRCLE

1. See André Malraux, *La Voie Royale* (Paris: Grasset, 1930).
2. Tzvetan Todorov and his 'hommes -récits' in *Poètique de la Prose*, p. 66

CHAPTER 8   TRIBAL AND ECONOMIC EXCHANGES

1. The butcher is quite (ir)respectfully considered by Conrad as being one of the two pillars on which society rests, the other one being the policeman (see 'Heart of Darkness'). So Winnie Verloc, who before meeting her husband had gone out with the son of a butcher, was no loser in the exchange, since she will 'butcher' her 'butcher' of a husband, treating him to a piece of cold roast beef, as cold as hatred (oh, the good old roast beef of England!) before plunging a butcher's knife into him. When that cunning bloodhound Chief-Inspector Heat smells the cold remains of Poor Stevie torn into pieces by the Greenwich explosion, law and order become olfactively perceptible through a nauseous domestic relationship.
2. T. S. Eliot *The Waste Land* (London, 1922).
3. Ibid.
4. 'Not with a bang but a whimper', T. S. Eliot, 'The Hollow Men'.
5. Gustave Flaubert in *La Tentation de Saint Antoine*: 'Je voudrais pénètrer chaque atome, descendre jusqu'au fond de la matière – être la matière!'
6. Michel Foucault in his Preface to Flaubert's *La Tentation de Saint Antoine* (Paris: Gallimard, 1967).

CHAPTER 9   MINING AND REFINING REALITY.

1. Virginia Woolf, *To the Lighthouse* (London: Hogarth Press, 1927).
2. D. H. Lawrence, 'The Woman Who Rode Away' (London: Heinemann, 1928).

CHAPTER 10   THE POWER OF WRITING

1. According Marlow's expression in *Lord Jim*. Everyone in *Under Western Eyes* uses this expression – there are so many of 'us'.
2. Scott Fitzgerald in *Tender is the Night* (1939).
3. See 'The Waste Land' a facsimile of the original manuscript edited by Valérie Eliot. (London: Faber and Faber, 1971).
4. We mean the author of *The Swiss Family Robinson*.

5. See Jacques Derrida *De la Grammatologie* (Paris: Editions de Minuit, 1967), translated as *Of Grammatology* by Gayatri Chakravorty Spivak (Baltimore: Johns Hopkins, 1976).

CHAPTER 11   CONCLUSION

1. Hegel, *La Raison dans l'Histoire*, Editions 10/18 (Paris: Union Générale d'Editions).
2. Hegel, *La Phénomènologie de l'Esprit* (n.d.), translated by Jean Hyppolite (Paris: Aubier Montaigne).
3. Ibid.
4. Joseph Conrad, *Under Western Eyes.*
5. Hegel, op. cit.
6. Joseph Conrad, *Letters to Edward Garnett* 1899. (Cf. *Letters from Joseph Conrad 1895–1924*, Edward Garnett (ed.) (Indianapolis, Ind.: Bobbs-Merrill, 1928).
7. Hegel, op. cit.

Bibliography

CONRAD'S WORKS

I have used the 1946–54 Dent edition of Conrad's novels, short stories and essays, focussing this study mainly on 'Youth' (1898), 'Heart of Darkness' (1899), *Lord Jim* (1900), *The Secret Agent* (1907), *Nostromo* (1904) and *Under Western Eyes* (1911).

I have also made borrowings from Joseph Conrad's letters especially his *Lettres Françaises* edited by Georges Jean-Aubry (Paris: Gallimard, 1929), his *Letters to Marguerite Poradowska, 1890–1920* edited by John A. Gee and Paul J. Sturm (New Haven, Conn.: Yale University Press, 1940), his *Letters from Joseph Conrad* edited by Edward Garnett (Indianapolis, Ind.: Bobbs-Merrill, 1928), and finally his *Letters to Cunninghame Graham* edited by C. T. Watts (Cambridge University Press, 1969).

BIBLIOGRAPHIES

Kenneth A. Lohf and Eugene P. Sheehy, *Joseph Conrad at Mid Century: Editions and Studies, 1895–1955* (University of Minnesota Press, 1957).

Bruce E. Teets and Helmut E. Gerber, *Joseph Conrad: An Annotated Bibliography of Writings about Him, 1895–1966* (Northern Illinois University Press, 1971).

The *Conradiana Review* has been publishing a 'continuing checklist' ever since 1972, *Conradiana*, Texas Tech University, Lubbock, Texas.

BIOGRAPHIES

Jerry Allen, *The Sea-Years of Joseph Conrad* (New York: Doubleday, 1965).

Georges Jean Aubry, *Joseph Conrad: Life and Letters*, 2 vols (New York: Doubleday, 1927).

Jocelyn Baines, *Joseph Conrad: A Critical Biography* (New York: McGraw-Hill, 1960).

Frederick Karl, *Joseph Conrad: The Three Lives* (London: Faber and Faber, 1979).

Bernard Meyer, *Joseph Conrad: A Psychoanalytic Biography* (Princeton University Press, 1967).

Ian Watt, *Conrad in the Nineteenth Century* (London: Chatto & Windus, 1980)

SELECTED STUDIES ON CONRAD

Jeffrey Berman, *Joseph Conrad: Writing as Rescue* (New York: Astra Books, 1977).

Jacques Berthoud, *Conrad: The Major Phase* (Oxford University Press, 1976).

Avrom Fleishman, *Conrad's Politics* (Baltimore, Md.: The Johns Hopkins Press, 1967).

Adam Gillion, *Conrad and Shakespeare* (New York: Astra Books, 1976).

——, *The Eternal Solitary: A Study of Joseph Conrad* (New York: Bookman, 1960).

Albert Guerard, *Conrad the Novelist* (Harvard University Press, 1958).

Bruce Johnson, *Conrad's Models of Mind* (University of Minnesota Press, 1971).

Eloise Knapp Hay, *The Political Novels of Joseph Conrad* (University of Chicago Press, 1963).

Camille La Bossière, *Joseph Conrad and the Science of Unknowing* (Fredericton, N. B: York Press, 1979).

F. R. Leavis, *The Great Tradition* (London: Chatto & Windus, 1948).

François Lombard, *Joseph Conrad: l' Aventure Métaphysique,* doctorate thesis, Rennes University, 1974.

Jean-Jacques Mayoux, *Vivants Piliers* (Paris: Julliard, 1960).

——, *Sous de Vastes Portiques* (Maurice Nadeau, 1981).

Thomas Moser, *Joseph Conrad: Achievement and Decline* (Harvard University Press, 1957).

John A. Palmer, *Joseph Conrad's Fiction: A Study in Literary Growth* (New York: Cornell University Press, 1968).

Claire Rosenfield, *Paradise of Snakes, An Archetypal Analysis of Conrad's Political Novels* (University of Chicago Press, 1967).

Norman Sherry, *Conrad's Eastern World* (Cambridge University Press, 1966).

——, *Conrad's Western World* (Cambridge University Press, 1971).

——, *Conrad: The Critical Heritage* (London: Routledge & Kegan Paul, 1973).

Edward Said, *Joseph Conrad and the Fiction of Autobiography* (Cambridge, Mass.: Harvard University Press, 1966).

Tony Tanner, *Lord Jim*, Studies in English Literature, no. 12 (London: Edward Arnold, 1963).

Dorothy Van Ghent, *The English Novel: Form and Function* (New York: Rinehart, 1953).

C. T. Watts, *Conrad's Heart of Darkness* (Milan: Mursia International, 1977).

Paul Wiley, *Conrad's Measure of Man* (University of Wisconsin Press, 1954).

Raymond Williams, *The English Novel from Dickens to Lawrence* (London: Chatto & Windus, 1970).

Morton Dawen Zabel, *Craft and Character in Modern Fiction* (New York: The Viking Press, 1957; first published 1932).

GENERAL BACKGROUND STUDIES

Roland Barthes, *Mythologies* (Paris: Le Seuil, 1957).

——, 'Les Sentiers de la Création Skira', L'Empire des Signes in (1970).

——,'Ecrivains de Toujours' in *Roland Barthes par lui-même* (Paris: Le Seuil, 1975).

Jacques Berque, *L'Orient Second* (Paris: Gallimard, 1970).

P. D Curtin, *The Image of Africa: British Ideas and Actions 1780–1850*, (London: Macmillan, 1965).

André Gide, *Voyage au Congo: Carnets de Route* (Paris: Gallimard, 1927).

Léon François Hoffman, *Le Nègre Romantique* (Paris: Payot, 1973).

Tim Jeal, *Livingstone* (London: Heinemann, 1967).

Pierre Jourda, *L'exotisme dans la Littérature Française depuis Chateaubriand*, 2 vols (Paris: Presses Universitaires de France, 1956).

Jacques Le Goff, *La Civilisation de l'Occident Médieval* (Paris: Arthaud Editions, 1964).

Michel Leiris, *l'Afrique Fantôme* (Paris: Gallimard, 1934). *Cinq Etudes d'Ethnologie* (Paris: Gonthier, 1969).

Claude Lévi-Strauss, *Tristes Tropiques* (Paris: Plon, 1955).

Alan Moorhead, *The White Nile* (London: Hamish Hamilton, 1960)

Pierre Yves Pétillon, *La Grand Route*, Fiction & cie (Paris: Le Seuil, 1979).

Jonah Raskin, *The Mythology of Imperialism* (New York: Random House, 1971).

Ronald Robinson, John Gallagher with Alice Denny, *Africa and the Victorians* (London: Macmillan, 1967).

Jules Saintoyan, *l'Affaire du Congo* (l'Epi, 1960).

Alan Sandison, *The Wheel of Empire* (London: Macmillan, 1967).

Leila Sebbar Pignon, *Le Mythe du Bon Nègre dans la Littèrature du XVIIIè siècle* no. 336, 337/338, (Paris: Les Temps Modernes, 1974).

Victor Segalen, *Notes sur l'Exotisme* (Paris: Mercure de France, 1955).

Michel Serres, *Jouvences sur Jules Verne* (Paris: Editions de Minuit, 1974).

A. P Thornton, *The Imperial Idea and Its Enemies* (London: Macmillan 1966).

Alfred Russel Wallace, *The Malay Archipelago* (London, 1894)

Index